COMPUTER-MEDIATED
ENVIRONMENT
AND LEARNER SUPPORT

COMPUTER-MEDIATED ENVIRONMENT AND LEARNER SUPPORT

Abed Salem

\<teneo\> // press

YOUNGSTOWN, NEW YORK

Requests for permission should be directed to:
permissions@teneopress.com, or mailed to:
Teneo Press
PO Box 349
Youngstown, New York 14174

TABLE OF CONTENTS

LIST OF TABLES AND FIGURE

PREFACE

Managers and instructors who know little about technology are
making decisions about the technology and tools for e-learning.
Information technologists make decisions without the benefit of
advice from practitioners in this field.

My study aim is to give teachers, trainers, instructors, educators, administrators, and instructional designers the knowledge
they need to use the tools and technologies that support learners
in an e-learning environment, and to use them effectively. It will
also help information technologists to understand the e-learning
tools that they could be asked to help select, combine, and use.

The Open University offers a Master of Arts Degree in Open
and Distance Education, which is open to postgraduate students
from countries around the world, and is delivered entirely online.
Students complete three 60-credit courses for the award of the
M.A., and they may study the courses in any order. For this case

study, I selected a 6-week block called 'Supporting Learners in ODL Systems', from the 9-month course on the 'Implementation of Open and Distance Learning'.

Forty students were taking this course. The students were divided into three groups, each with their own tutor and learning environment. My group comprised 12 mature adult learners from different countries and from different backgrounds and professions. Learners could post messages to the other groups, as well as within their own group.

The learners' perspective is particularly relevant at a time when universities and colleges are expanding their involvement in the delivery of online courses for on-campus and distance learners. The boundaries between the conventional educational setting and the online environment are increasingly blurred. In this case study, I set out to evaluate, illuminate, and bridge a gap in our understanding of an online learner-support system system.

Learner support does not take place in a vacuum; a learner-support system should operate in four dimensions—the organisational, social, pedagogical, and technical dimensions. We can compare it to the four wheels that support a car and enable it to move forward. It is important to establish a balance among the four dimensions of learner support. Like a car, any weakness in one wheel (dimension) would adversely affect the performance of the car (organisation), the passengers (students), and the drivers (staff).

I examined a range of variables that affect a learner-support system, by reading and analysing messages posted to the conference area, and by reflecting on my own experience as an observer and as a participant in the group under study.

With careful planning at the early stages of course design, a learner-support system can play a significant role in improving students' learning outcomes. One size does not fit all, and some customisation may be necessary to meet the needs of a particular student. This is especially important at a time when the learner-centred approach is paramount.

Education providers and students alike are looking for innovative teaching and learning solutions. Above all, they are looking for solutions that they can control, customise, and roll out. The in-depth analysis in this study provides evidence that a well-resourced and well-supported learning environment offers opportunities for students with different styles of thinking and learning to express themselves.

ACKNOWLEDGMENTS

In writing this book, I would like to acknowledge support and encouragement from my tutors, Molly Cumming, Dr June Mitchel, Mr Ian Smith, Dr Rae Condie, Dr Mary Thomson, Dr Rebecca Soden, Dr Ian Finlay, Prof Gilbert MacKay (Reviewer), Dr Erica McAteer (Feedback), and Dr Margaret Kirkwood (Supervisor). Many thanks to my supervisor who provided me with wonderful ideas, comments, energy and support throughout the last four years of my study. I enjoyed working with you, sharing ideas, having discussions and guidance.

I would also like to acknowledge the support and encouragement from Marilyn Lister, Chris Kennedy, who have contributed in one way or another towards editing, proofreading, editing, encouragement, and support.

I owe special thanks to my wife Catherine and my two children Diana and Kareem for being there, all these years. Their patience and support, especially relieving from many of the house duties, was a bonus towards writing this thesis. To my family, I dedicate this thesis.

COMPUTER-MEDIATED ENVIRONMENT AND LEARNER SUPPORT

CHAPTER 1

INTRODUCTION: COMPUTER-MEDIATED ENVIRONMENTS (CMEs) AND LEARNER SUPPORT

1.1. THE RESEARCH CONTEXT

The government intends that its policies on using computer-mediated environments (CMEs) will widen participation, increase pedagogical access and flexibility, and strengthen the learning process by stimulating a higher quality of instruction.

Colleges and universities are well placed to respond to these aspirations by embracing e-learning technologies, because most governments want to raise the education level and skills of their population. E-learning has the potential to transform education at every level; it can make a high-quality educational experience available and extend access to those whose location and economic and personal circumstances have prevented them from pursuing educational goals in the past. These learners also represent a wider student market for universities and other educational institutions. The common objectives of these institutions are raising quality and standards, meeting diverse needs, widening participation, building skills for employability, and motivating learners to develop new skills for the 21st century.

The rapid expansion in the use of CMEs over the last few years has challenged higher education institutions to support learners' increasingly diverse needs with innovative approaches to enhance the quality of the learning experience. However, the government objective, 'to fully embed e-learning in a sustainable way within the next 10 years' (HEFCE, 2005, p. 2), has put an additional strain on tight budgets, as institutions seek to use more e-learning infrastructures (HEFCE, 2003). Tutors have experienced increased stress; they need to develop new skills in using CME with distance learners while using their computer skills during traditional classroom instruction. CME place new demands on organisational, social, teaching, and technical skills.

Academic institutions are seeking ways to expand their curriculum base, increase enrolments, and reduce costs simultaneously. Many institutions have adopted new techniques in communication, information technologies, and services. There are attempts to support educational activities by linking students with their peers and instructors in CME (Hiltz, 1994). System designers and programmers need to develop technology-mediated teaching environments that deliver a high standard of education regardless of time, place, and access.

Learning management systems, learning-content management systems, authoring tools, and collaboration environments are evolving rapidly. Tutors using e-learning systems now have a much greater choice of hardware and software, but this may have increased the overall complexity of the selection task. Course tutors are not software experts; they need a systematic way to identify the tools they need, as well as a means of evaluating various products.

Learner support in CME is a complex matter that merits detailed consideration. Until recently, academic institutions placed relatively little emphasis on teaching learners how to use the tools and features within CME. Moore and Kearsley (1996) suggested that one reason for this could be a belief that installing servers that are more powerful and posting courses to the Web will automatically improve the quality of teaching and learning:

> A common misconception among educators who are not familiar with a systems approach is that it is possible to benefit from introducing technology into education, without doing anything to change the other ways in which education is currently organized. According to this view, once technology is in place, there is little else to be done except to let teachers get on with practicing their craft as they have always done. (p. 6)

However, the technical solution is insufficient by itself. In my view, there is also a need to assess the effectiveness of online-learning environments.

In the last 10 years, rapid advances in information technology and increased functionality on the intranet have helped universities, colleges, and other education and training establishments to widen access to education and improve the quality of their courses. Software tools tailored to the particular needs of learners are the principal means of communication. The two-way computer-mediated communication systems (CMC) used on academic Web sites offer new opportunities to access knowledge and exchange information. However, the belief still persists among some educators that once they have posted online courses onto the Web, they need do nothing more to support the learning process or to deliver the same standard of learning experience that students would find in a classroom.

Distance education practitioners have recognised that because online learners are separated from their teachers and are isolated from their peers, they need different methods of support. In response to the needs of a remote audience, academic staff are designing Web sites and putting their lecture notes onto the Web so that students can browse and hold e-mail discussions about them. Increasingly, the software industry is developing innovative software to support online courses. Despite the variety in design, style, complexity, and costs, these systems are insufficient to support quality teaching and learning. Educators need a new frame of reference—a systems approach that will provide an adaptable structure.

Current and past research on CME has focused on technical applications rather than offering any deeper consideration of the teaching and learning process. In my opinion, an overemphasis on the technology has diverted attention from the all-important social and cognitive interactions.

There is evidence that online learning using technological tools has not produced the desired high-quality results. Many educational institutions that were using only conventional face-to-face teaching methods have invested heavily in technology as a response to government policies on embedding technology into teaching and learning. However, they have paid little attention to the structural, cultural, and financial prerequisites for online learning.

This is possibly due to poor understanding of distance learners' needs, since technological tools alone are unlikely to facilitate quality teaching and learning. The lack of adequate support strategies has contributed to the failure to produce good results. A CME needs support strategies that provide reliable online system availability, good design, and high-quality communication and interaction.

The HEFCE E-learning Strategy review (HEFCE, 2003) contains this aim: 'To contribute to the understanding of issues posed by e-learning, evaluate good practice, disseminate this and reflect it in the review of the strategy and future strategic direction' (n.p.). The review acknowledges the following:

> We do not yet fully understand all the impacts that new technologies may have on learning and teaching; and we do not fully understand the needs of learners and employers in respect of technology-supported learning...We believe therefore that a strand of our strategy must be analyzing and building upon existing research evidence, to improve understanding of the issues that underlie future e-learning development. This will need to include evaluation of innovative practice, and its impact on the effectiveness of learning for learners and employers. (n.p.)

Academic institutions are making more use of technology to expand learning opportunities, and this trend is likely to continue. In this context, it is vital to prepare learners for the experience of learning through a computer-mediated environment. Irrespective of the tutor's expertise in his subject area, he will need to understand how to use a CME for instruction and how to apply techniques that will help students to reach the expected learning goals. According to Hawkridge (1995),

> Learner support, an integral part of a computer-mediated environment in a collaborative learning environment, is a developing area of practice and research. It is in the

descriptive phase of theory development and there are numerous variations in media, interaction, interface design, as well as pedagogical factors, which need to be examined. (p. 85)

The challenge for the instructor in supporting the learner through CME is to devise ways for the learner to use the online tools effectively. Clearly, there is a need for research into innovative practice in CME, where the boundary between teaching and supporting learners becomes blurred.

1.2. THE RESEARCH OBJECTIVE

My research objective was to identify the effective practices for supporting student learning within a computer-mediated environment. My research evaluates innovative practice; it demonstrates the importance of this topic and contributes to academic knowledge about learner support. The central question I ask is this: How can tutors use the specific elements of CME and other interactive technological features effectively, to support the known learner or a group of learners? This question leads on to several subsidiary questions at an empirical level:

- Why is learner support important?
- What contribution does knowing one's learner make to learner support?
- How do course design strategies affect learner support in a CME?
- What choice of media and technologies should tutors make available in a specific learner-support system?
- What makes for an effective learner-support system in a particular context?

I contend that these elements are dynamic and bespoke, rather than fixed. Although CME have become part of the academic landscape, a literature review shows that there is relatively little research on recommended practice where courses are using CME exclusively. Perhaps this is because CME are new to academic institutions, especially those of dual mode, or because this is a relatively new and complex topic. This study examines a course block at the Open University (Unit H804), focusing on

    a.   tools and features in a computer-mediated environment;

    b.   learners' and tutors' discussions and insights about a learner-support system, from messages posted into the support area; and

    c.   the technical and administrative support made available to students and staff.

1.3. Defining a Computer-Mediated Environment

Most definitions of computer-mediated communications (CMCs) explain CMC as a pattern of communication. Romiszowski's definition of CMC (Khan, 1997) includes 'any form of organized interaction between people, utilizing computers or computer networks as the medium of communication' (pp. 32–33). Although this describes the communication among individuals within an online environment, it places little emphasis on the 'computer networks', the components that drive the communication process, or the mechanisms that are used to support learning. This definition fails to consider how 'organized interaction' occurs, or the methods, processes, and behaviours that participants need in order to facilitate organised interaction.

My search for a definition of CME did not identify a suitably comprehensive definition in the literature. I would define CME as all those elements of an open- and distance-learning (ODL) system and other interactive technological systems that are capable of responding to a known learner or a group of learners. Open and distance learning refers to forms of organised learning based on the physical separation between the learners and those involved in the organisation of their learning (Tight, 1988), and where learners are able to learn at the time, place, and pace that satisfy their circumstances and requirements (Manpower Services Commission, 1984).

I suggest that CME is a useful umbrella term that subsumes CMC, virtual learning environment, Web-based system, and computer-based instruction as a form of guided human-to-human communication-supported technology. I would also include in this definition the interaction factor between the user and the package contents—interaction with online text, books, video clips, animation, graphics, images and audio clips.

1.4. DEFINING LEARNER SUPPORT

There are claims that learner support within CME is synonymous with face-to-face learner support. McMann (1994) pointed out that CME tutors perform a similar role as the traditional face-to-face tutor. Nevertheless, I have identified significant differences right from the start of an online course.

Distance tutors require different methods and skills from than do engaged in conventional tutorial practices. Some academics view learner support as a substitute for any weakness in the teaching design or materials, while others regard it as essential to effective teaching and learning. Thorpe (2000) argued that regardless of whether one views learner support as remedial, it must be embedded into open- and distance-learning (ODL) courses. Thorpe defines learner support as 'all those elements of an ODL system capable of responding to a known learner or group of learners' (p. 51).

This broad definition emphasises the interaction between individuals who know each other, but it does not consider the guided interaction needed to meet the curriculum aims and objectives. Thorpe (2000) also stops short of including the features of interaction found in software and multimedia packages. I would expand this definition of learner support to include 'all those elements of an ODL system *and other interactive technological features* [italics added] that are capable of responding to a known learner or group of learners' (p. 51). In my view, learner support is not only about the interpersonal interaction that takes place using a CME; it also includes software and hardware features designed specifically to facilitate and enhance learning support.

The European Computer Driving Licence (ECDL) is a good example of these technological features. The main study guide for students who enrol on the ECDL programme is a CD-ROM. The course consists of seven modules, which students work through using embedded interactive features such as audio, animation, demonstration, and interaction. The combination of technological features and guidance from the course team allows students to go through the material at their own pace and to reach a successful conclusion.

1.5. WHY CME MERITS INVESTIGATION

Although distance-learning methods are widely used around the world, research into online and distance education still lags behind other areas of research (Perraton, 1995). Moore (1995) suggested this is due to the absence of a theoretical underpinning for research, the failure to refer to previous research, and poor research design. The same is true of research into learner support.

There are a few references to distance learning and learner support in journal articles and reports, and some references scattered through books. However, most of these references are general analyses of the origin, definition, history, and development of distance education, and there is no focus on specific issues. Many writers in this field deal with broad topics in distance learning and education, such as access, evaluation, systems for providing feedback to students, and quality-management issues. Hawkridge (1995) made one of the few attempts to expand the research. He proposed a draft agenda for the evaluation of distance education, and suggested priorities for course content, media choice, and student support. There is little research on recommended practice for delivering online courses.

The selection of any precise research problem depends largely on why the research is undertaken. The purpose of my research was to bridge the knowledge gap and provide a framework for understanding the importance of learner support in a CME. My study should facilitate understanding of the process of creating frameworks for learner support in a CME. It provides insights into ideas for recommended practices in learner support, which should have relevance for CMEs across the educational domain.

Several logically interrelated issues shaped my approach. The starting point is the pedagogical focus, which considers how to apply learner-support practices in institutions delivering online learning. This includes content analysis and interpretation that could be useful to decision makers, administrators, students, technicians, and teaching staff who wish to extend their understanding of online learning. In particular, I explain the features of design and the tools that include the learner in a learner-support system. My second aim was to provide insights into the kind of knowledge that learners engage in, the pedagogical practices, and the relationship between academic staff and the learners. I undertook this study to answer this question and to provide an insight into the challenges and opportunities in designing computer-mediated learner-support systems.

1.6. My Interest in Learner Support and CME

I have been involved in learner support in a CMC environment for 15 years. My interest in this field dates back to 1988, when I developed a virtual learning environment named 'Nosy', in order to supplement and enhance learning support for face-to-face and distance learners.

'Nosy' included most of the interactive features used today in similar systems. An important feature in 'Nosy' was the conference area, an interactive asynchronous feature, which functioned as the hub of learner support and allowed the reading and writing of messages independent of time and place. My experience of developing and using 'Nosy' led me to become a practitioner in this field.

In 1998, I studied for a M.A. degree in Open and Distance Education at the Open University (OU) Institute of Education. The course comprised of four compulsory units: H801 (Foundations of Open and Distance Education), H802 (Applications of IT in Open and Distance Education), H803 (Dissertation Module), and H804 (Implementation of Open and Distance Learning), which the university delivered entirely online, using a CME and an eBBS.

The emphasis for H801 was on a printed text box, while H802 used books and the online environment. The emphasis for course H804 was the online environment. For example, the University delivered the 'Learner Support' topic entirely online. Students discussed the topic through an eBBS, facilitated by a tutor. The participants shared their experiences and reflected together on the work of practitioners in ODL and on learner support. The main reason I chose to examine the OU course for this book was to highlight the roles of the participants involved in a CME. I contend that it is possible to have subject experts, quality material, and a state-of-the-art computer-mediated environment, but still fail to use this environment effectively to deliver courses.

When I spoke to many students and tutors who had used CME at different academic institutions, their comments were mainly negative. Some students felt that they had received no support at all, and as a result, they were unsure how to set about finding out what to do. Tutors had posted course materials onto the network without signposts to tell students what to expect, or what tutors expected from them. Other students had disregarded the lack of signposting; they felt that the course material was all they needed to learn and to take an exam at the end of the course. Some of the tutors who taught online were unsure about their roles. These observations, and many others, were the driving force behind my desire to illuminate what learner support is about, and how to facilitate and evaluate its components.

There are existing studies on the successful use of computer-mediated communication (CMC) in supporting learners in their own professional environments. Harasim (1999) studied a Dancing in Cyberspace course, in which 35 dancers and dance students from Spain, France, the United States, and Canada all signed up for the online choreography course. Mason (1998a) evaluated CoSy, a simple bulletin board used to deliver an Open University online course.

My study examines the effective use of Computer-Mediated Environments (CME) for online learning, networking, and teaching in the context of Open University course H804, 'The Implementation of Open and Distance Learning'. I contend that an effective approach requires a learner-centred focus, taking into account the practitioners' views of learner support in open and distance learning. I concentrated on a particular 6-week period when the students were discussing 'learner support in Open and Distance Education', partly because of the importance of learner support in a computer-mediated environment, but more importantly because I believe that this study will yield to a richer understanding of what learner support means in a computer-mediated environment.

1.7. THE BACKGROUND TO OPEN UNIVERSITY COURSE H804

The university-designed course H804 is for managers, administrators, and decision makers working in an education establishment. A postgraduate qualification was a prerequisite to course entry. Most of the cohort of 40 students on this course had already completed courses H801 and H802 and had experience with online learning. The student cohort was divided into three groups, each of which had their own tutor and learning environment. There were 12 mature students in my group, from different countries and with different backgrounds and professions.

The course comprised four blocks, each of which had a set of readings followed by online activities. Unlike most Open University courses, the largest portion of this course was in digital format, with supplementary study material in the form of print, audiocassette, and videotapes. An experienced, computer-literate tutor delivered the course, provided support, marked assignments, and moderated the online environment. The tutor was a former student who had experience of using the software and the conference area.

Students were required to have a personal computer, a modem, and an Internet connection in order that they could comment in the conference area on issues arising from the written or digital material. Learners could simply observe communications on the conference area, or post messages to their group or other groups, if they wished. Students' contributions to the conference area accounted for 10% of the work. At the end of each block, students submitted an assignment electronically to the Electronic Marked Tutor Assignment (ETMA) server. Tutors marked the work and returned it to the service, with feedback for students to download.

The course support team comprised a chairperson, a technician, an administrator, and the librarian. The chairperson's responsibilities were to certify compliance with Open University (OU) policies and to ensure the quality of the learning processes within the online environment. The chairperson's support duties included

- drafting the agendas for developmental meetings, in consultation with tutoring and support staff;
- monitoring participants' contribution behaviour within the virtual learning environment to ensure that it was consistent with the university rules and policies and those imposed on it from outside partners and stakeholders;
- ensuring that meetings and deliberations were fair, open, and thorough;
- making all interpretive decisions that fell within the topics covered by the university policies; and

- negotiating with participants on an acceptable format for topics, threading, and message sharing.

The main duties of the technician allocated to the CME were to assist the information-technology staff in responding to the computing needs of the learners on and off campus. This included, but was not limited to, hardware and software installation and troubleshooting hardware, software, and connection problems.

The administrator who was allocated to the assembly provided advice on managing the learning environment and implementing key course policies. He acted as an intermediary between the management and the teaching and support staff. He was responsible for reducing any barriers and constraints limiting online use, such as communication networks, equipment problems, and access to resources.

A librarian provided online resources related to the course material, collated specialised information to be posted to the Web, and supplied online requests for journal articles and conference papers. Participants were also given access to the International Centre for Distance Learning (ICDL) Web site, a comprehensive online searchable database of resources on distance learning courses/programmes offered by Commonwealth institutions.

At different stages of the course, tutors introduced an 'ask an expert' thread to the conference area in order to engage with students on and from different viewpoints. This feature was intended to supplement the tutors' expertise and bring an extra motivational dimension to the learning process. The concept has some resonance with marketing and personal empowerment, and it has proved to be a good motivational technique. In this context, it connected the student more directly to issues by bringing different perspectives to the learning. For example, if the guest was the author of the topic under discussion, students had an opportunity to argue and debate directly with the author and become motivated towards a deeper approach to learning.

The communication system comprised e-mail, computer conferences, assessment server, libraries, and storage to support the teaching. A graphical user interface was the primary means of entry to the course area, and it had good access and navigation features. Postal and telephone contact were available.

1.8. THE RESEARCH DESIGN

I have based this study on the hypothesis that we know little about the processes of designing a learner-support system as it occurs within a real-world context. Consequently, we have little understanding of how best to provide adequate provisions to support it. We therefore need better ways to conceptualise design strategies within the context of its use.

Collaboration plays an important role in learner support, where dialogue is an essential ingredient in the making and exchange of meaning. Harasim, Hiltz, Teles, and Turoff (1995) presented CMC as a new paradigm for collaboration, which offers unique opportunities to respond to distance learners' needs in an environment that tutors can tailor to specific needs.

Much of this study revolves around the strengths and weaknesses of CME in learner support. I have adopted a topical approach based on the Systems Model for Distance Education (Kearsley, 1996). I have described the main support processes for the learner in a CME, paying particular attention to the learner profile, interface, course design, the support teams, and multimedia as a way to make learning accessible and easy to implement. I have described, explained, and evaluated learner support in a particular CME that engages distance-learning students, even when their contact with the institution is entirely through the Internet, by post, or by telephone. I do this by examining the experience of using CME through the voices of decision makers, students, and staff. I illustrate various points of practice to support my recommendations of good practice.

Parlett and Hamilton (1977) advocate a holistic view, 'illuminative evaluation': 'The aims of illuminative evaluation are to study the innovatory program: how it operates; how it is influenced by the various school situations in which it is applied' (p. 1). I have taken this holistic view of learner support in CME in order to examine what is on the surface and to explore the underlying issues. A holistic perspective is important when examining an innovative program, rather than just concentrating on individual components. A holistic view of learner support in a CME takes into account the learner, the academic institution, and government policies, rather than focusing simply on one symptom or a part that has a problem. In advocating this perspective, I contend that the overall result can be greater than the sum of the individual components.

> A holistic view of e-learning should lead to a methodology, which is open ended and empowering enough to allow the learners to be the ones who highlight the issues which are important to them…There is an opportunity to design the forthcoming research study so that it is able to shed light on the learner intentions and rationales behind commonly noted observable behaviours. (Sharpe, Benfield, Lessner, & DeCicco, 2005, n.p.)

- During the 6 weeks in which this learning block was open to students, the participants—course tutor, students, lurkers (students from other groups on the course), and guest speaker—exchanged messages through the electronic bulletin board,[1] as part of their study to work individually and collaboratively on a block activity titleld 'learner support' issues unique to this situation was that

a. the MA in Open and Distance Education programme was designed with professional educators in mind and hence the students were professionals representing educational organisations, research establishment, and adult-learning institutions; and

b. the topic the students were debating as part of their formal study was the topic of 'learner support'.

The main elements are source, design, delivery, supporters, front-line supporters, and interaction. I explored how these components work together to provide a suitable platform for a learner-support system. My research involved an analysis of the learner profile, the learning environment, course design, media selection, feedback, and interaction.

Allowing the learners to be the ones who are voicing the issues of learner support in a computer-mediated environment provides valuable, rich data to the e-learning community. My approach identifies issues and questions that should bridge the gap in our understanding of learner support and learner needs.

1.9. CHAPTER SUMMARY

In this introductory chapter, I have highlighted the rationale for a learner-support system in a computer-mediated environment. The provision of learner support is implicit when students attend a structured course in an educational institution. There has been a steady expansion in learning at a distance from the educational institution. Many of the barriers that prevented adults from accessing further learning opportunities in the past have been removed. Therefore, the need for learner support has become even more important in distance-learning programmes. This has led me to consider the structures needed to help practitioners and educational institutions adopt effective learner-support systems.

ENDNOTE

1. A bulletin-board system (BBS) is software that permits remote users to connect to the network that runs the system. The BBS provider supplies log-on information, and the user connects to the BBS through a modem or on broadband. Once inside the environment, users can exchange messages, read news, and have asynchronous discussions with other users.

CHAPTER 2

BACKGROUND

2.1. CHAPTER OVERVIEW

This chapter reviews the literature on computer-mediated environments (CME) and learner support. I have based my approach on the framework for e-learning (Khan, 2005), focusing on four dimensions that are critical to the design of effective learner-support systems: the institutional, social, pedagogical, and technical dimensions. This approach covers the principal themes and issues in students' experiences of learner support in a CME.

2.1.1. Defining Learners

I have used the terms 'students', 'learners', and 'practitioners' interchangeably in this study. I refer to individuals enrolled on H804 as students; I regard them as learners because they are adults, and as practitioners because they are professionals in

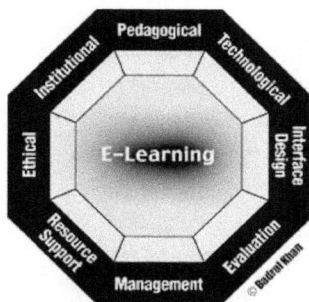

Reproduced with permission from Dr. Badrul H. Khan.

the field of online and distance learning. I have used the terms 'learner experiences', 'learner voice', 'learner reflections', 'learner insights', and 'learner perspective' interchangeably to represent the learners' own words, because this study focuses on what they are saying about learner support in a CME.

2.1.2. Defining Learner Support

Robinson (1995) identified three definitions of learner support:

1. all the online distance learning (ODL) elements that can respond to an individual student,
2. the support embedded within self-learning material, and
3. the support services essential to the successful delivery of the learning experience.

The range of services included in a learner-support model will vary according to the context. Robinson emphasises the dynamic nature of the interaction among learners, their peer contacts, and feedback systems, and with support services such as support material and access to study centres, libraries, laboratories, and equipment.

2.2. THE IMPORTANCE OF THE LEARNER'S EXPERIENCE

Increasingly, organisations concerned with the policy, funding, delivery, and quality of e-learning are recognising the importance of learners' own experiences. Most studies of CME examine course design and programme-focused teaching methods; there are few research reports on the requirements for effective learner-support systems. There is a need for student-focused studies that use students' own descriptions of their experience of learner support, or that capture their perspectives on their needs and on how organisations support these needs. There are four possible reasons for the dearth of research on learner support (Robinson, 1995):

- academics may see learner support as less glamorous than other activities in distance and open learning;
- learner support may be seen as peripheral to the 'real business' of developing materials;
- learner support can be particularly vulnerable to budget cuts; and
- learner support may be largely a pragmatic activity, rooted in the lessons of experience.

The Joint Information Systems Committee (JISC) has a mission to provide excellent leadership in the innovative use of Information and Communications Technology to support education and research. The JISC-funded 'E-Learning and Pedagogy' programme is addressing these issues with practitioners from the JISC community, asking the following:

- How can we enhance current knowledge about what constitutes effective practice in e-learning?

- How can we support practitioners with their use and understanding of e-learning?
- How can we promote the development of terminology and frameworks that will improve understanding and sharing of practice in e-learning?

The 'Learner Experiences of e-learning' module within the Pedagogy strand of the E-Learning Programme[1] seeks to ensure that learners' needs are central to the design and development of learning technologies and their applications. An exploration of this theme engages a wider spectrum of the educational community in discussions on the learners' voices; the aim is to 'identify effective approaches to e-learning practice'.[2]

The JISC 'Learner experience of e-learning' (LEX) project aims to put learner voices at the centre of the research study. This study is part of the pedagogy strand of the e-learning programme, and builds on a recently completed scoping study and literature review. This suggests that there has been little research on learner experiences, and this provides a starting point for my research: 'the experts in learner experience are the learners' (Mayes, 2006).

I begin with an examination of the literature that addresses these questions:

1. What is the justification for the choosing 'Learner experience'?
2. Why is the 'learner experiences' voice important to teaching and learning?
3. What is the justification for learner support?
4. Why is learner support important to teaching and learning?

2.2.1. The Justification for Researching the 'Learners' Experiences'

Increasingly, research suggests that bringing learners' voices to the fore can benefit learners, tutors, the institution, and the system as a whole; the best way to understand learners' needs is to examine them through the learners' own words. Failure to listen to learners risks increasing their disengagement and isolation, which is a common reason for student dropout. Fielding (2004) suggested that eliciting the learners' voices will show that researchers take their views seriously:

- A focus on the learners' voices will reveal the intricacies of individuals' experience, which should help academics to understand this meaning and significance within the teaching and learning context.
- Learners will feel respected; they will see how their views translate into positive outcomes for both their personal learning and for the educational establishment.
- Learners will be more inclined to reflect and discuss their learning, and this should stimulate the production of the tools to influence what, where, and when they learn.

2.2.2. Why the 'Learner Voice' Is Important to Teaching and Learning

Giving practitioners' voices centre stage provides rich opportunities to develop CME and ensures real benefit to the learners. The Department for Education and Skills (DfES) acknowledged this tacitly, in its recently published e-strategy on harnessing technology[3]: 'We need to listen to people's views and ensure that the technology meets their needs'. This suggests the need for a more integrated, cross-sector approach. Morgan (1995) stated, 'The basic tenet of this book is that understanding learning from the learners' perspective is the crucial starting point for our work as teachers, trainers, and course designers in improving student learning in open and distance learning' (p. 11).

2.2.3. What Is the Justification for Learner Support?

The term 'learner support' covers a range of diverse practices; it reflects local cultures and institutional differences. Some people see learner support as a remedial activity that is necessary because of weaknesses in teaching design or materials; others regard it as an effective tool for teaching and learning (Thorpe, 2000).

Regardless of whether learner support is remedial, it needs to be included as part of learning in a CME. Others working in the distance education field have seen learner support as the unfortunate survival of face-to-face teaching. Mills and Tait (1996) attributed the weakness of learner support to the dominance of managers:

> The increase dominance of managerialism in the educational context, driven by a broad socio-political environment which concretely demands 'more for less' in an environment of rapid technological change, is reviewed in terms of its tendency to diminish the potential for student support to embody the processes and values of conversation and community. (p. 60)

There are three generations of distance education (Nipper, 1989). The first generation used correspondence teaching based on printed material. The second generation used on multimedia: television, radio, video, and audiocassettes. The third generation (as in the H804 course) now uses computer-conferencing systems. Each generation uses media devised in earlier generations. The expansion from the early days of correspondence courses for home study to the flexibility of 21st century distance learning demands a shift from a producer-centred, tutor-led focus to a learner-centred approach.

2.2.4. Why Is Learner Support Important to Teaching and Learning?

As academic institutions compete to deliver online courses in the Internet marketplace, they need to include excellent learner-support systems as part of their offering. Distance-education providers, such as the Open University in its early days, relied heavily on the quality of print-based media; they had little interaction with their learners. The availability of high-quality material from a range of new providers has now removed the competitive advantage that universities enjoyed formerly because of their high-quality course materials (Latchem & Lockwood, 1998). Learner support has become a critical success factor for providers of open and distance learning.

There are three reasons why learner support is important (Thorpe, 2000):

- it involves interpersonal interaction, which is one of the most important means through which people learn,
- it has a direct effect on the efficiency and effectiveness of ODL systems, and
- it is the focal point for many of the current changes in information-technology applications.

Hill (1997) defined learner support in terms of four dimensions: organisational, social, pedagogical, and technical. The common factor in these four dimensions is the interaction and collaboration between:

- instructor and instructor,
- learner and instructor,

- learner and learner,
- learner and content,
- learner and administration, and
- learner and interface.

Information technology and communication theorists suggest that, despite the possible difficulties associated with interaction and collaboration in Internet-based courses, fitting the medium to the appropriate learning model can help to enhance interaction. However, other researchers suggest that instructors need to learn a different set of teaching skills for the transition to a new role as facilitators and moderators (Brandon & Hollingshead, 1999). A more conversational style in offering comments online encourages student participation and discussion (Ahearn, Peck, & Laycock, 1992).

The emphasis on dialogue as a constructivist approach to learning within a community of practice shifts the focus away from the traditional instructivist, teaching-centred approach. The new model operates in a context of socially bound communication based on seeking, sharing, and making meaning of knowledge. Instructors need to emphasise the importance of interaction and collaboration in Internet-based courses, as well as the methods that the tutor needs to facilitate them.

There is evidence that the instructional design used in most distance-education institutions has relied on a behaviourist approach, which focused on the effectiveness of instruction for the learner, rather than learner-effectiveness for instruction. This approach links closely to the Fordist principle of offsetting the high production costs of material in education against the number of students:

> It must be of concern that so many recent converts to distance education view it in Fordist terms as a

low-cost, high-volume application of technology to the delivery of knowledge. Whatever the merits of the Fordist debate, it is no accident that experienced practitioners expected to extol the virtues of new technologies are more apt to surprise their audience by focusing instead on course design, student support, and a critical perspective. To do otherwise would be to ignore the lessons of the past three decades of distance education. (Paul & Brindley, as cited in Mills & Tait, 1996, pp. 47–48)

Followers of the Fordist principles believe that offering Internet-based courses with broad appeal to thousands of students over several years will enable educational institutions to survive. On the other hand, post-Fordists believe that the future of distance education will lie with 'niche courses' for a smaller number of students, such as the H804 course. Smaller educational institutions, moving more quickly and with smaller investments, may be more agile in responding to the changing market. Converts to distance education should listen to experienced practitioners in open and distance education, and learn lessons from the past.

Distance education is shifting from being 'producer-centred' to 'learner centred', largely because of a change in consumers' expectations (Rowntree, 2000). This shift necessitates different approaches and guidelines for learner support in order to enhance the quality of teaching and learning.

2.3. THE ORGANISATIONAL DIMENSION

The organisational dimension of the e-learning framework includes policies relating to learning, course planning and preparation, course marketing, preenrolment information and advice, and Web-site production, maintenance, and materials (Hill, 1997).

These elements are closely related to the learner profile, orientation to learning, and the student's approach to learning.

2.3.1. Knowing Our Learners

The overview essay 'Knowing our learners in ODL' (Rowntree, 1987, p. 8) provides the starting point for this section of the literature review: Rowntree asks: 'what do we know about our intended or intended learners—e.g. What are their needs, expectations, and circumstances?' Rowntree attributed the need to know about these learners to the following:

    a.   a shift in learning from being producer centred to learner centred,

    b.   a shift from selling (producer-oriented product) towards marketing (consumer-oriented product),

    c.   a shift in society from seeing learning as 'preparation for life' to 'learning *for* life', and

    d.   a shift from a product orientation to a customer orientation.

Organisations that are unfamiliar with open- and distance-learning systems will find that they need to make fundamental changes to their policies, procedures, applications, and implementation. This requires knowledge and understanding of the learners' characteristics, which translate into support needs once the student commences the learning process.

Knowing the learner at an early stage of the course, or even before the course or programme starts, provides the course team with opportunities to identify objectives, recognise the needs of the learners, and select the right context and level of support that is likely to promote effective learning (Rowntree, 2000):

> Clearly, there are many things we might need to know about our learners, and it would not be idle curiosity. The fact is

such knowledge could have far-reaching implications for our teaching. It could certainly help us decide what kind of course and support system we need to develop to meet learners' needs. Without it, we cannot be sure of providing them even with what they would see as relevant learning experience, let alone the satisfying one. (p. 20)

In future, educational institutions will face an increasing diversity of students with varied learning needs; they will need to make the adjustments necessary to enhance students' outcomes. The management and administration of a distance education programme is complex (Moore & Kearsley, 1996). There are administrative barriers at four levels (federal, regional, state, and institution), which might influence how the institution implements policies and how it budgets its resources for staffing, scheduling, and quality assurance. Moore and Kearsley provide a list of events and activities that institutions should embrace in order to manage and administer the teaching and learning in distance education.

In response to the shifts discussed above, Thorpe (2000) listed areas in which learners may need support; she begins with the question 'who are your learners?'. Thorpe suggests that the first stage is to profile the prospective learners, in order to find effective supports for their learning.

The Learner Profile
The learner profile is a central consideration for online learning, as it helps learners to understand other students and to interact more efficiently. Educators should consider many questions about the learner profile before and during the design and development of online courses:

- Who are they?
- Where do they come from?

- What gender are they?
- What subject knowledge do they possess?
- What are their learning styles?
- What are their orientations to learning?
- What is their approach to learning?

The diagram in the appendix provides an overview of the complexity of the learner profile. For example, knowing the age of the prospective learners may affect the design, presentation, and teaching style of the course, the student motivation, and the level of support needed. The 'third agers' are becoming increasingly active in online learning (Bilston, 1989). It is generally accepted that we are less likely to retain information as we age; compared to younger learners, older learners may need more time to complete the course. Learners access resources in diverse ways, and this will affect course design and delivery. Failure to take account of these factors will lead to a course that is overloaded, poorly timed, and too expensive (Rowntree, 2000).

Orientation to Education
Orientation to education encompasses how and why learners engage in education and tackle their work in a particular way and the reasons and attitudes behind this. There are three principal orientations: personal, vocational, and academic; Morgan (1997) suggested that each of these can be divided into intrinsic, extrinsic, and social orientation.

Learners bring to their engagement with learning a diverse inventory of differences in past educational experience, expectations, fear, lack of confidence, physical accessibility, IT skills, and social and emotional problems. Acknowledging the learners' diversity will help course designers and teachers to understand the obstacles learners face when they tackle their work. If they take a cause/effect approach to understanding learners' orientation, it will help them to improve students' learning. Course designers and teachers need to promote a positive motivational context, a high degree of learner activity and interaction with others, and a well-structured knowledge base.

Concepts of Learning

If education is the transmission and acquisition of knowledge and understanding of our world through the study of art, culture, history, languages, music, philosophy, and so on, then learning is the acquisition of knowledge in an educational context to a certain standard of achievement.

The Learner profile illuminates how learners think of learning. Morgan (1997) identified five qualitative concepts:

- learning as the increase of knowledge;
- learning as mere memorisation;
- learning as an abstractions of meaning;
- learning as the acquisition of facts, procedures, and so on, which can be retained and/or used in practice; and
- learning as an interpretative process aimed at the understanding of some personal reality.

Understanding these concepts and representing the various ways that learners view their studies is an important stage in developing the learners and engaging them in a meaningful way.

Motivation

Motivating is especially important in open learning, and motivating the learner should be one of the prime concerns from the start of the course. Bligh (1972) suggested that six things motivate students:

- the desire for relevance,
- curiosity,
- enthusiasm from the lecturer,
- the need for social interaction,
- achievement and fear, and
- activity and esteem.

These six motivators apply equally to online learners; students like their studies to be relevant to their preferences. Understanding learners' preferences will help course designers to devise practical activities that provide experience relevant to the students' needs. Studies have shown that students' learning and interest improved if tutors asked questions and engaged them in discussion rather than simply giving them facts. An online environment can provide a suitable platform for arousing curiosity and stimulating dialogue and interaction if a tutor initiates a discussion by posing a question and inviting discussion in the conference area.

Some students are naturally enthusiastic about learning, but many expect their tutor to inspire, stimulate, and challenge them. Beard and Senior (1980) suggested five orientations for students' motivation:

- vocational,
- academic,
- social-intellectual or liberal,
- nonconformist or reformer, and
- collegiate or social-fun.

However, Adar (1975) suggested that four particular needs drive a student's motivation:

- the need to achieve,
- the need to satisfy one's curiosity,
- the need to fulfil one's duty, and
- the need for affiliation.

Morgan (1997) concluded: 'The main point is that the amount of effort students put in to studying, and how that effort is directed, is logical in relation to their individual aims and purposes in being in higher education' (p. 48).

The Approach to Learning

Learners approach learning in different ways. Morgan's (1997, p. 72) adapted summary of Ramsden noted that learners may take either a deep approach or a surface approach:

Deep approach	Surface approach
• Relating ideas together • Identifying main points • Constructing meaning • New material evolves through destruction and construction of material • Focusing on argument • Identifying internal emphasis • Relating concept to everyday experience	• Memorisation • Reproduction of information (copy and paste) • Focusing on assessment • Lacking confidence

The deep and surface approaches to study correlate with motivation: 'deep' with intrinsic motivation and 'surface' with extrinsic motivation.

There is evidence to suggest that assessment methods can encourage surface learning, and some learners become too focused on assessment and may 'miss the point' of learning. Some students will get to know the system and will work only to meet the minimum requirements. Many university students have been 'coached' by their tutors to get the grades they need to get into next course or level. Rowntree (1987) has questioned the effectiveness of assessment:

> The traditional three-hour examination tests the student's ability to write at abnormal speed, under unusual stress, on someone else's topic without reference to his customary sources of information, and with a premium on question spotting, lucky memorisation, and often on readiness to attempt a cockshy at problems that would confound the subject's experts. (p. 135)

2.3.2. Who Decides What Learner Support Is Required?

E-learning strategies aim to facilitate teaching and learning for a diverse group of learners who are studying at a distance through computer-mediated communication systems. A poorly managed e-learning system can lead to a high dropout level. A common mistake that providers of e-learning make in adopting new technology is to package and distribute courses or programmes without recognising the accompanying management, administration, learner-support, staffing, and resource issues (Paul & Brindly, 1996).

The type and scope of the online-learning programme will determine the extent and complexity of these issues. Moore and Kearsley (1996) identified seven areas of management in distance education programmes: policy, planning, budgeting, staffing, resources, scheduling, and quality assessment. They suggested that highly skilled specialist teams should create the online courses. However, the larger the number of participants, the more costly the production becomes; more resources are required in order to improve quality outcomes.

Lockwood (1995) listed four common political and economic agendas that have a direct impact on government support for distance learning:

- access and equity,
- economic development and workforce training,
- improving the cost effectiveness of education and train- ing, and
- improving the accountability of the education system.

Selecting the appropriate hardware and software requires more than funding; careful planning and skilled decision making are important for success. However, '[t]he undisputed technical advantages of making information more easily and more demo- cratically available are to some extent undermined by human skill limitations on effectively using such an information net- work' (Romiszowski, 1997, p. 32).

Rossner and Stockley (1997) emphasised the need for coordi- nation in creating the technological vision within the education sector. The process will require

- support from senior administration levels;
- a campus-wide IT backbone to access Web-based instruction;
- library facilities online;
- student registration via the Web;
- access by student/faculty to any campus-based server containing relevant information supporting research in hardware, software, modes of instruction;
- input from existing faculty/technical people with techni- cal knowledge;

- developing support systems to provide training in the educational uses of interactive technologies; and/or
- the provision of ongoing technical and pedagogical support to both faculty and students, committing adequate budget.

Senior management needs to look at broader trends and issues in the transition from face-to-face instruction to online learning. These managers are responsible for innovation and they acquire funding, look for new partners, and make decisions about support strategies (Collis, 1997). The transformation requires a mix of persuasion, rational argument, and powerful leadership.

2.3.3. Who Provides the Support in a CME?
Thorpe (2000) stressed the importance of establishing good interpersonal communication between the learner and the supporters, and identifies various roles in learner support, including tutor, chairperson, conference moderator, mentor, advisor and counsellor. This list can shrink or expand, depending upon the context. Moore and Kearsley (1996) used the terms 'Guidance and Counselling' for learner support at various stages: these terms relate to problems with health, family, jobs, course selection, media selection, and study approach.

The Tutor
The tutor plays an integral part in course delivery by providing a stimulating environment that is conducive to students' learning and meets their expectations. This role is not simply about creating and posting material to the Web, but also about creating learning situations in which learners actively engage in making meaning of learning. The ability to create a friendly online environment for learning is an essential skill for the tutor.

Freeman (1997) suggested that the tutor has five main functions in most systems:

- as a subject expert,
- as a gateway to other resources,
- to give feedback on progress,
- to encourage/assist with personal problems, and
- to assess learners.

He suggests three additional roles (set up the role, manage and support the role, evaluate the role) to support these functions.

Tutors working in a CME environment have a specialised role because online activities generate the learning; they are enablers who are skilled in group building and organisation, and they need to stimulate as much interaction as possible among participants (Mills & Tait, 1996). The student needs enabling tutors to stimulate conferences, summarise wide-ranging views, provide new topic areas where discussions and interactions go off track, and stimulate new strands, themes, and approaches. Tutoring skills related to group building and maintenance become important. The tutor typically undertakes 'weaving' the student contributions together, for example, collecting up statements and relating them to concepts and theories taught in the course and to forthcoming assignments. Collis (1997) referred to a tutor as an instructor, but finds it difficult to define his/her role in a CME:

> The instructor may no longer be involved in the design or its instructional balance, but be primarily focused on the roles of communicators and motivators...the converse may also be the case, as well as combinations of both design and delivery aspects. (pp. 353–354)

Aalto and Jalava (1995) saw the tutor's task as actively tracking and supporting the students' learning process. They emphasise dialogue as a means of promoting understanding and helping the students in adapting new ideas and approaches that enrich their experiences: 'The task of the teacher is to support and to actively follow the student's learning process. The Key word is dialogue, i.e. the interaction which takes place in the learning environment' (p. 259). The tutor's communication skills, self-confidence, ability to guide and support the individual student, knowledge, and practical skills in managing groups are essential ingredients to support the students' learning.

Focusing on these competencies from theoretical and empirical investigation and personal experience led Baath (1980) to place the tutor at the centre of student learning:

> This is the role of the distant tutor: he can have important pedagogical functions, not only that of correcting errors and assessing students' papers. He may play a principle part in the linking of learning materials to learning—by trying to relate the learning material to each student's previous reinforcement patterns (Skinner), or to his mathemagenic activities (Rothkopf), or to his previous knowledge and cognitive structure (Ausubel), or to his previous comprehension of the basic concepts and principles of the curriculum (Bruner), or by concentrating on the task of establishing good personal relationship with the learner (Rogers)—as I have tried to demonstrate. (p. 33)

Thorpe (1994) used the terms facilitator and tutor interchangeably. She argues that the facilitator needs to know the material in order to support the learners. She provides a list of course-briefing requirements that a facilitator should fulfil as a starting

point for his/her teaching. However, Mills and Tait (1996) expanded
the facilitator's role to include writing the course materials:

> There is an immediate opportunity for students to be in
> contact with the academic staff who have written the
> courses and with all other students and the tutors. At first
> sight, this seems to be a real step forward, providing easy
> links between student and course author. (p. 19)

Tutors are normally involved in developing teaching material to
support the learners' needs. Lockwood suggested that staff training and development is a necessary prerequisite to support this
process, and proposes a board game for this purpose (Latchem &
Lockwood, 1998). Rowntree (1995) recognised that tutors teaching online may not possess all the technical skills they need to
work successfully; they may help from technical staff.

The Chairperson

The chairperson is normally a subject expert whose duties are
to ensure the integrity of the learning process within the online
environment. On occasion, he or she may contribute directly
to the line discussion area by posting a message, for example,
regarding events such as inviting an expert to the conference
area. Having a chairperson on the course provides a quality
component; students feel more confident knowing that there is
more than one official person communicating with them.

The Conference Moderator

Thorpe (2000) defined the conference moderator as a skilled
person who ensures that the online medium is effective for
learning. A good discussion does not 'just happen'. The conference moderator's role includes initiating interaction, monitoring
conference attendance, encouraging students' participation and

contribution, and monitoring and processing the content of the discussion. Thorpe suggests that the tutors can absorb and carry out these skills. She also reports that students felt a sense of group belonging and engagement in interaction when the moderator is skilled in communicating his/her personality through onscreen text, e-mail, and conferencing.

The Mentor

Mentors are trusted advisors and helpers who guide the learners to people who can answer their enquiries. Thorpe (2000) identified mentors as established experts. Mentoring should enhance rather than diminish the expert role of the teacher. Mentors are usually faculty members who are masters of access and assimilation and have direct experience of the course (Glennie, in Mills & Tait, 1996, p. 19). Mentoring is likely to take place when students request it, or when it is apparent that they need mentoring support. Mentors should help students with their study problems and contribute to strengthening the cognitive structure that students acquired from previous learning. I believe that mentoring should be integrated into the support system regardless of other variables, and that mentors should be specialists in the field.

Depending on the size and context of the online course, tutors may find themselves taking on more than one role. This may be feasible on a very small scale, for example, with a group of 15 students. However, as student numbers increase it will become necessary to assign roles to specialists in each field. (Peters, 1998). Freeman (1997) saw the role of the Mentor as that of an experienced tutor who provides support and advice to new tutors, who 'may have no day-to-day contact with other open tutors and so have few opportunities to share their worries or pick up tips' (p. 48).

The Advisor

The Advisor acts as just-in-time support to the learners' needs. For example, s/he provides information on course choices. Cochran-Smith (1995) reflected on the role of an advisor in learner support:

> David Smith: It's stunning to me that no one talks about this stuff! In college, I didn't have a single advisor who encouraged me to take a Black History course. Not one! And that blows me away! Because I wasn't going to do it on my own. I did not have the background that would say, 'Go take a Black History course'. But if an advisor had sat down and said, 'I think you'd really benefit from this and I think you'd learn a lot'...These articles are just blowing me away! I wonder where they've been all my life, you know? (p. 541)

The Counsellor

The counsellor provides a learning path to the student and helps to solve problems. The counsellor and the learner may work together according to a draft plan through which learners develop their knowledge and self-judgement. For example, students may experience communication problems with other students or tutors, or struggle with writing online comments and work for assessments. The counsellor may direct students to Web links that may help them to improve their writing skills.

2.3.4. Course Information and Administration

A 'course' can be defined as the package of material or services and the benefits that learners will derive from studying the programme. Freeman (1997) listed what a prospective student might ask:

- Does the course match my need?
- Am I ready to take the course?

- What will I learn?
- What will studying the course involve?
- Over what period can I take the course?
- How will I be able to get help?
- What will I need to provide?
- What will be provided for me?
- What will it cost?
- Will I get qualification?
- What will the course enable me to do next?

Mason (1998b) suggested criteria that can help prospective learners make an informed decision about enrolling on a course: the course aims and objectives; the delivery medium; and the course cost. Clearly, the course syllabus should set out the course aims and objectives, course entry prerequisites, fees, guidance, assignment details, and arrangements for learner support.

Administrators act as intermediaries between the management and the teaching and support staff to reduce the barriers and constraints that students may face, including barriers and constraints in using the technology and accessing the resources (Donaldson, 1990). Moore and Kearsley (1996) provided administrators and instructors with a list of what students expect from a distance education program: up-to-date course information; courses that accommodate a flexible learning style; feedback on their work and progress; and help in dealing with administrative problems related to the program. They note that colleges and universities may find that institutional policies and administrative procedures designed for traditional on-campus learners may not work for an online system.

Gagne, Briggs, and Wager (1992) described the administrative information as 'external' events of instruction necessary to support 'internal' events of learning that prompt students to make appropriate strategic adjustments fitting to the task and the expected outcomes. Haughey and Anderson (1998) stressed the importance of developing online systems that are comparable to conventional systems for registering students, collecting tuition fees, completing grant certificates, submitting records of examinations, and managing the other activities necessary to support the learner.

2.3.5. Staff Development
One of the shortfalls for conventional colleges and universities offering online courses is the lack of skills and approaches in planning, implementing, and organising staff development within the e-learning domain. Taylor (1997) recognised that

> [t]raining is now recognised as a critical ingredient of all successful industrial enterprises, whether local, national or global. Capitalising on the human resource potential of employees is becoming even more critical as we encounter the trends towards rapid developments in technology, globalisation, knowledge-based organisations and the attendant emergent need for lifelong learning. Ensuring that employees acquire expertise in a range of complex tasks quickly and effectively is now an essential organisational objective to generate and maintain a flexible, competitive workforce. Achieving this objective in a cost effective manner is critical to sustainable economic and social development. (n.p.)

Staff training and development plays a vital role in helping staff acquire the knowledge, skills, competencies, and dispositions that they will need in a CME. Approaches can include workshops, on-the-job development, a tutor handbook, and online training. Freeman (1998) called for a written standard for staff who manage the quality systems. Rowntree (1998) suggested the need for a staff-development strategy throughout the life of a project.

On-the-job development involves providing support in aspects directly related to the work in which the staff are involved. For example, new tutors at the Open University are assigned mentors who are, according to Sewart (1998), experienced lecturers who provide informal peer support during the course. Freeman (1997) found that the commonest approach in offering tutors guidance on administrative aspects is the tutor handbook. Online training provides opportunities for staff who enjoy this mode of learning or are physically separated from those who are delivering the training. A CME is the best fit for online training where knowledge building is strengthened through the sharing of ideas, skills, and information among the participants (Harasim et al., 1995).

2.4. THE SOCIAL DIMENSION

Learning is inherently communicative; it is our innate propensity to enquire and our desire to know that lead to the creation of communities:

> Far from being elitist, this notion of learning rests simply on the assertion that, as Aristotle said, all human beings by nature desire to know, and the more Socratic view that no one finally knows and the very possibility of knowing expands with a community of enquirers. (Mandell & Herman, 1996, as cited in Mills & Tait, p. 5)

When people talk about online-learning environments, they usually assume that students will learn by themselves, in their own homes, or in other environments. The commonly stated advantages of online learning (students able to work at their own pace, anywhere, and at any time) imply that the learner is working alone. Many online-learning providers find it difficult to understand learners' needs fully.

Online-learning environments, as well as formal-learning environments, have recognised the value of peer-learning situations in which several students work together. The lack of a physical presence in a CME does not prevent people from sharing their experience through conversation and discussion (McLellan in Khan, 1997). Collaboration and interaction between individuals with complementary skills create new learning. McLellan draws on Schrage's Model of Collaboration, Communities, and Values in Internet-based education; an important aspect of this model concerns integration, mutual respect, tolerance, and trust. Occasional problems with extraneous variables such as gender, mistrust, intolerance, different abilities, and race can interfere with communication and collaboration. McLellan recognises that 'the Internet is not a panacea, but it can filter out some "noise" factors that interfere with communication and learning' (p. 189).

Malikowski (1996, p. 287) acknowledged that physical presence has an important value in social interaction, especially when students can only communicate with one another through a computer screen. He contends that interactive video, audio, and chat can reinforce cohesion in the class. Establishing a Web page where students post their biographies with photos and e-mail addresses with introductions about themselves tends to help to social integration in a CME (Bates, 1995, as cited in Malikowski, p. 288).

Wegerif (1998) identified the importance of including the social dimension in the course design in order to increase the effectiveness of online learning. His study demonstrated the importance of the social dimension to collaborative learning, using a threshold measure as a bridge between 'outsiders' and 'insiders'. 'Outsiders' were those students who failed to learn and were unable to cross the threshold and become 'insiders'. Several factors account for this failure, including 'course design, the role of moderators, the interaction styles of course participants and features of the technological medium used' (p. 1).

Evans (1997) has identified other factors that are likely to influence learners: money, sex, power, age, work, and leisure. His exploration of the learners' unique world, in the learners' own words, exposes the frequent (but misguided) assumption that students are a homogenous body. He reflects on a range of educational and social backgrounds, presenting them as stories by people studying different courses. These diverse backgrounds present open and distance educators with a complex challenge: 'Adult learners en masse are every bit as difficult to understand and predict and yet we need to do so with a reasonable degree of certainty to be good educators' (p. 128).

Romiszowski (1997) discussed the interrelationship among technology, changing social and work structures, and the need for changing education and training paradigms. He defines the knowledge worker as 'somebody who earns a living by using knowledge in order to create new knowledge' (p. 25). There is a need for a systems analysis of the 'end product' with a new type of 'knowledge work' that is characterised with interaction, not only with content, but also with conversations between networks of people with a common interest.

2.5. THE PEDAGOGICAL DIMENSION

2.5.1. Pedagogical Philosophy

Smith and Ragan (1997) suggested that '[i]nstruction is the delivery of information and activities that facilitate the learner's attainment of intent, specific learning goals' (p. 5). Hannum and Briggs (1982) suggested that all 'traditional instruction' takes place within an instructional environment that encourages passive learning, ignores students' individual needs, and ignores problem solving and intellectual skills. Web-based instruction is a unique domain of instruction, which requires a different approach to teaching and learning than do conventional classroom pedagogies; it is also different from traditional approaches to distance learning. Two schools of thought have emerged about learning theory and approaches to Web-based courses: the Instructivist and the Constructivist (Gillani & Relan, 1996).

Instructivist

Instructivists stress the importance of defining objectives; they contend that learners acquire knowledge through truth, using the senses, and that knowledge can be tested precisely. Learning is built through an unstructured sequential process, a hierarchy from lower level to higher order. Hence, objectives are achieved through sequential process. With a sequential process there is no structure. Structure depends on three components: Sequential, conditional and looping. Bonk and Reynolds (1997) provided a range of instructional strategies, which can be directive for Web-based instruction. These include brainstorming, creative writing, role-play, metaphorical thinking, and many others.

Constructivist

Constructivists believe that learners construct meaning from experience in a learning environment, which should therefore be rich and diverse. The tutor provides and orchestrates the richness of the learning environment. Constructivists advocate these principles for a learner-centred approach:

- provide experience of the knowledge-construction process,
- embed learning in realistic and relevant contexts,
- encourage ownership and a voice in the learning process,
- embed the learner in a social experience,
- provide experience in and appreciation of multiple perspectives,
- encourage the use of multiple modes of representation, and
- encourage self-awareness of the knowledge construction process.

A learner-centred constructivist approach seeks to empower the learner with the necessary media tools that will transform them from a passive, static audience into active and productive participants. To constructivists, the learner is like an active internal database with a personal representation of knowledge, which is indexed by his/her experiences.

The constructivists' approach to design gives the learner the opportunity to synthesise, organise, and restructure information and to create new information. Knowledge and its construction should be dynamic, active, and innovative, which contradicts with many current assessment systems.

2.5.2. The Virtual Learning Environment
The pedagogies for computer-mediated learning aim to facilitate and support a pedagogically sound and accessible learner-focused approach. The widespread use of virtual learning environments in colleges and universities has led course designers to demand

better design and higher standards in pedagogic technologies that will support effective practice.

Planning is the first stage in developing Web-based information for an online course.

According to Ritchie and Hoffman (1997), instruction involves the following:

- motivating the learner,
- specifying what is to be learned,
- prompting the learner to recall and apply previous knowledge,
- providing new information,
- offering guidance and feedback,
- testing comprehension, and
- supplying enrichment or remediation.

Deciding on the technology and media at early stages of the design process identifies the scale support that might be necessary to help tutors and learners. According to Khan (1997),

> Web-based instruction (WBI) is a hypermedia-based instructional program which utilizes the attributes and resources of the World Wide Web to create a meaningful learning environment where learning is fostered and supported... WBI students can interact with each other, with instructors, and online resources. Instructors and experts may act as facilitators. They can provide support, feedback and guidance via both synchronous and asynchronous communications. (p. 6)

A CME offers appropriate support tools for collaborative and team working. Tutors, administrators, consultants, and editors— who are working as a team for a project and who may come from different countries—will benefit from a well-defined networked support infrastructure, which follows the same infrastructure described by Kaye (1992):

> Adopting a standard software package for writing and publishing electronically, such as Microsoft Word. Hosting a conference and e-mail system such as eBBS (Electronic Bulletin Board System) network access from offices (both on the central campus and from regional offices) is readily available, as is related technical help access from home is available at local telephone call rates via a large number of dial-up nodes throughout the UK (these dial-up nodes currently serve over 2500 students and tutors on courses using the eBBS conferencing system and other online facilities, and the Academic Computing Service provides help services for such home-based users). (p. 12)

2.5.3. The Tutor's Role in a CME

Paulsen (1995) saw the tutor's role as goal setter, discriminator, host, pace setter, troubleshooter, entertainer, lecturer, tutor, facilitator, mentor, and mediator. According to Harasim et al. (1995),

> A learner-centred (rather than teacher-centred) model has been found as the best fit online. CMC is meant for the sharing and building of ideas, information, and skills among the participants to strengthen knowledge building, integration, and application of conceptual information. (p. 24)

Harasim argued that any collaborative learning carried out using peer interaction, or collaboration where the role of learner support is shared between learners themselves and their tutor, requires at least some monitoring and structuring that is integrated within the support of the facilitation of learning.

Rowntree (1995) divided the tutor's role into four main areas: organisational, structural, social, and conceptual:

On the organisational level: the tutor ensures that students have the right equipment, passwords, access to administrators and technicians, and so on.

On the structural level: the tutor plans the overall content and structure of the course—the topics to be covered, aims and objectives for each topic, the mode of collaboration (individual, group), the timetable, learning resources, assignments, and deadlines.

On the social level: tutors act as hosts to the learning event, mainly through text and where visual and auditory cues are missing:

> So the tutor needs to take a lead in setting the tone of the discourse, establishing an etiquette, promoting mutual respect between participants, defusing personal antagonisms, discouraging the formation of cliques, counselling offended individuals, and generally making sure that disagreements do not go 'over the top'. (Rowntree, 1995, p. 213)

Feenberg (1989) also endorsed this role:

> As social host s/he has to issue warm invitations to people; send encouraging private messages to people complimenting them or at least commenting on their entries, or suggesting what they might be uniquely qualified to contribute. As meeting chairperson, s/he must prepare an enticing-sounding initial agenda; frequently summarise or clarify what has been going on; try to express the emerging consensus or call for a formal vote; sense and announce when it is time to move on to a new topic. (p. 214)

On the conceptual level: the tutor's concern is to ensure that the course participants enhance and deepen their understanding, and can apply the concepts from the course.

Holmberg (1988) positioned conversation as a metaphor for educational relationships, where 'feelings of personal relation between the teacher and learning parties promote study pleasure' (p. 116). While Holmberg stressed the personal relationship between the tutor and learner, Moore (1993) proposed a theory of transactional distance, which includes 'instructional dialogue'—where the term dialogue carries a considerable degree of purposefulness that is 'valued by each party' (p. 31), as opposed to the broader term of interaction. Moore's learners are treated with respect, and their role as students is not diminished by one another and cannot be diminished by the tutor or the institution.

In the context of making the learning pleasurable and purposeful, dialogue requires a knowledgeable and competent facilitator (Berge, 1995). The tutor's competence is comparable to a salesperson who knows the product they are selling very well—but this is not enough to make the sale. The salesperson needs skill in selling techniques and customer relations in order to close the sale.

Feenberg talks about how message topics and threading in a CME help to support the tutor in guiding the learning:

> [R]eview printouts, harkening back to earlier discussions, clarifying confused expressions, identifying the themes, making connections...Such weaving comments supply a unifying overview, interpreting the discussion by drawing its various strands together in a momentary synthesis that can serve as a starting point for the next round of debate...they allow online groups to achieve a sense of accomplishment and direction. (1989, p. 214)

Paulsen (1995) provided useful general guidelines for moderating educational computer conferences. He called on moderators to reflect on their preferred pedagogical styles based on their philosophical orientation and facilitation techniques. Mason (1991a) identified four basic functions that a moderator must posses for successful conferencing: organisational, social, pedagogical, and intellectual.

2.5.4. Support for Tutors in a CME

The level of support a tutor might need relates closely to the job description. Freeman (1997) gave a sample job description, which states that the tutor will 'be responsible for designing, delivering and administering a professional and quality service of agreed and development related activities on behalf of the Open College over a contracted number of days per year' (p. 76). Tutors play a major role in a learner-support system:

- Pedagogically, they facilitate the building, scaffolding, and weaving of the online community through the initiation of start-up dialogue, assigning tasks and activities, providing sign posts and anchor points, directing learners to external resources, summarising key points, keeping the discussion on track, weaving together various discussion threads, maintaining harmony and connectedness among learners, and providing a dynamic scaffold among the groups.
- Socially, they provide a user-friendly interactive environment, and supportive and responsive to learners' circumstances.
- Managerially, they manage the learning environment, such as dividing the learners into small groups and acting like a football referee by providing a set of rules and protocols, maintaining interaction protocol, and managing and assessing the learner progress.
- Technically, they provide navigational support in liaison with Web master technicians and administrators.

In addition to their skills and experience as subject experts, course tutors need to be able to use the technology to deliver the course. The assumption that every tutor with basic computing skills will be able to use the virtual learning environment effectively is false.

Educational institutions need to decide what they require from their tutors, how to support them effectively, and who will be responsible for each aspect of support. Freeman's multistage development scheme for new tutors is a useful starting point for determining the level of tutor support. Evidence that suggests that lecturers lack online support: a survey by NATFHE, the university and college lecturers' trade union, has revealed a lack of technical support. The survey showed that 87% of lecturers in colleges and universities are using some form of online learning, but there is a lack of training in online teaching techniques, and little extra time is available to help the lecturers develop material and online teaching techniques (www.natfhe.org.uk/down/onlinelearn.pdf).

Thorpe (2000) summed up the complexity and diversity of a learner-support system and gives tutors useful pointers on pre-emptive approaches for tackling various learner problems such as lack of self-esteem, work pressure, and so on.

2.5.5. Learning Styles
The rationale for embedding different styles of presentation in a computer-mediated system is to provide learners with choice and flexibility. Learners differ in the way they think and how they process information. Honey and Mumford (1986) have identified four distinct learning styles:

- Activists get on with a given task straightaway, often progressing by trial and error.

- Pragmatists plan and enjoy the practical application of ideas, have great attention to detail, and present in a clear and rational way.
- Reflectors take time to work systematically in a structured and often highly innovative and creative manner.
- Theorists produce organised, well-structured work, showing considerable attention to detail.

Learners will have preferred learning styles and cognitive modalities (a preference for visual, auditory, or kinaesthetic); they will respond better to modes of delivery that suit their preferences (Dunn & Dunn, 1993). There are also different thinking styles (Jonassen & Grabowski, 1993) or fields of dependence and independence that can be divided into two subdimensions: autonomy of interpersonal relations and cognitive restructuring

Knowing learners' preferences should help course designers to produce material for online delivery that will suit diverse needs. This will involve the selection of suitable practices, based on the perceptions of the learners' needs, the nature of the learning environment, and on how the tutors intend to maximise the learning outcomes. Rowntree (2000) asked: 'If you are developing an ODL programme that must suit all learners' (p. 18) what do you do to make it:

- novel and participatory enough for the activists,
- intellectually rigorous enough for the theorists,
- practical enough for the pragmatists, and
- leisurely enough for the reflectors?

Course designers need an established procedure for assessing the learners' needs and their preferred learning style before the course starts. Profiling the learners at an early stage should ensure that the institution matches the prospective learners to the most suitable type and level of course and provides them with appropriate resources.

2.5.6. Collaboration and Collaborative Learning

> Collaboration is the process wherein Units work together to achieve outcomes for shared stakeholders, quicker and more cost effectively than if they worked on their own, without having to change the 'how' codes of any of the participating Units. ('collaboration', 2007, n.p.)

This definition echoes Thorpe (2000), who defined learner support as 'all those elements of an ODL system capable of responding to a known learner or group of learners' (p. 51).

The process of collaboration has four properties:

- Situation is where people know each other and share similar interests.
- Interaction is where dialogue and conversation take place, using asynchronous or synchronous forms of communication to exchange and share knowledge.
- Mechanism is where specific roles are assigned in order to bring about more intrinsic collaboration.
- Measure is where the effect of collaboration is evaluated.

From a constructivist perspective 'collaboration emphasises interaction among the individuals as situated activity, depending on several social elements that are integral to effective and sustained communication' (Lave & Wenger, 1991, p. 61). Lave and Wenger advocated discussion and dialogue as a constructivist approach to learning within a community of practice. They emphasise the learner-centred approach, which requires the group to function as social actors connected through discourse in a context of socially bound communication based on seeking, sharing, analysing, organising, and exchanging insights.

Collaborative learning refers to various instructional practices that encourage individuals to work together as they apply course material to answer questions, solve problems, or create a product (Colbeck, Campbell, & Bjorklund, 2000). There is a strong emphasis on group organisation in collaborative learning. Koschmann (1996) referred to collaborative learning as 'a commitment to learning through doing, the engagement of learners in the cooperative (as opposed to competitive) pursuit of knowledge, the transitioning of the instructor's role from authority and chief source of information to facilitator and resource guide' (p. 13).

Harasim et al. (1995) highlighted the potential benefits of collaborative learning in promoting deep learning and social cohesion. However, there are also potential problems with levels of participation, transactional costs, assessment, and interpersonal conflict. For, example, a group member who takes little part in the activity may still receive the same grade as others who made greater efforts in tackling the activity. Collaboration implies that all participants equally contribute to a solution. This suggests that a group working together may require some kind of social contract between peers or between peers and the tutor. This contract would specify the conditions under which collaborative tasks can progress.

The interactive many-to-many nature of conversations in a CME assumes that all participants have equal say and that their voices should be heard. Learning in a CME constructivist context is a social-dialogical process where interaction between group members facilitates meaningful learning. The extent to which these processes function effectively depends upon the degree of symmetry in the group interaction:

- Symmetry of action is the extent to which the same range of actions is permitted among participants (Dillenbourg & Baker, 1996).
- Symmetry of knowledge is the extent to which participants posses the same level of knowledge, which reduces hierarchy, control, and authority.
- Symmetry of status is the extent to which participants have similar interest with respect to their community.

Group members in a CME have equal opportunities to contribute to the discussion. Students who may have found it difficult to speak up in face-to-face classes—because of language differences, feeling intimidated by others, or for other reasons—can take time to draft a thoughtful, written reply.

CME should provide a democratic platform in which participants have equal access to the discussion regardless of race or gender. However, Herring (1993) identified social-gender bias in CME electronic conferencing, where men tended to speak up more often and more aggressively, and women used passive language and more deflection. Several complex variables may influence equal-opportunity issues within a CME. Juler (1998) proposed a discourse model and identifies two issues that affect the interaction among participants:

> The discourse model, as I have proposed it, contains the possibility of what I call 'asymmetry' since at any conference there may get notable scholars invited as keynote speakers or simply as worthwhile participants, and at time they will probably seem to dominate the formal proceedings...On the other hand, there are all the other

activities both formal and informal in which, for the most part, there can be much greater symmetry. Discussion groups, for example, will usually, be chaired by someone who attempts to ensure equal opportunity for all to participate, and on less formal occasions it is very much up to each individual to make the effort to join in. Nevertheless, the very weight of some people's reputation may be enough to intimidate those with less experience and so prevent them gaining from these opportunities of interaction.

Rosenberg and Sillince (2000) identified four dimensions that may give rise to asymmetry:

- the introduction of new knowledge: which may clash with given knowledge;
- the degree to which the group's knowledge exchange clashes between the ideal and real dimensions, which may cause the suppression of new ideas;
- power and hierarchy—where those on the peripherals are suppressed and marginalised; and
- the degree to which the communication is task oriented— which is influenced by the 'cluelessness' of the communication medium (e.g., an online group discussion is more task oriented than conventional group discussion).

Promoting symmetry within a CME is not an easy task. Recognising the complexity of this issue and raising awareness of the problems that could arise from discussions within a CME is a positive step in establishing a platform for effective teaching and learning.

The desire to move students from information user to information producer has been a dominant theme in education reform over the last decade, taking students from passive observers to active participants (Hedberg, 1997, as cited in Khan, 1997, p. 47). The overarching goal is collaborative learning; students are encouraged to participate in the learning by creating an environment that primarily 'involves students in doing things and thinking about the things they are doing' (Bonwell & Eison, 1991, p. 28–34) and gains them new knowledge through dialogue with others (MacConnell, 1992, as cited in Mills & Tait, 1996, p. 90).

However, the learner-centred approach, where the student takes 'control' of his or her own learning, has blurred the defined roles of the tutor and student; it has created conflicts that affect the outcome of collaboration. Therefore, some form of protocol is needed to enhance collaboration, and this is especially important in a CME, where the normal voice tone and visual cues are missing. A basic collaborative-learning dialogue model, the 'empathy templates' formed from a set of phrases, is designed to avoid bad feeling caused by a breakdown in interaction among participants (Zimmer, 1995, as cited in Lockwood, 1995, p. 149). However, Zimmer noted that not enough importance is placed on the empathy template:

> The relative scarcity of empathic comprehension inviting warm affirmation (C-IA) in all of the support-element profiles may reflect a widespread cultural deficiency. People simply are not aware of the 75 percent chance that their clear understanding of what someone has said actually is wrong. (as cited in Lockwood, p. 149)

Earlier investigations into the psychology of acquiring knowledge focused on the processes. There has been little research on how individuals represent their knowledge (Jeong & Chi, 1999).

How learners influence the learning outcomes of their learning partners is an important issue in the literature on cooperative learning (Tudge, 1989). Assuming that a range of different resources is available (prior knowledge, contextual information, resources to use, task schedule, task approach, etc.), the group develops a specific pattern of resource use that is conducive to their learning (Rogoff, 1991). Several studies show that team members converge on a similar conceptual model during collaboration; this can increase team efficiency and develop the shared knowledge needed for successful collaboration (Klimoski & Mohammed, 1994).

2.6. THE TECHNICAL DIMENSIONS OF LEARNER SUPPORT

Computer-Mediated Communication is about learning and not about technology. Berge (1996) asserted, 'I want to emphasise in the strongest way that when developing and delivering instruction, whether online or not, the use of technology is secondary to well-designed learning goals and objectives' (p. 22). Understanding the learning context and students' access to resources is critical for planning and delivering online courses. Rowntree (2000) put this very plainly:

> Learners may differ markedly in how much access they have to computers, workshops, libraries, other learners, workplace, mentors, supportive manager and colleagues, and so on. If you don't take such factors into account, you could end up (as providers sometimes have) with a course that is overloaded, too expensive, badly timed, and based on media inconvenient for learners to use, and facilities they can't get access to—in short, unsuited to their circumstances. (p. 21)

2.6.1. Access to Resources and Support

The current problem with technology is that it is insufficiently transparent and easy to use for students and tutors. Learners are concentrating too much on learning the technology and not enough on the course itself. Even the best computers are susceptible to crashes and malfunctions. Implementing a computer-mediated system requires careful planning and sustainable support. Changes in technology and media demand new skills and techniques. On one hand, technicians need more training when new technologies appear on the scene, and on the other hand, they need to liaise effectively with front-liner users (tutors, administrators, assessors) and make sure that they have the right equipment and that everything is configured correctly in order to communicate with the central computer and the students (Rowntree, 2000).

Haughey and Anderson (1998) noted that many learners are novice computer and network users, and some need a great deal of technical support to allow them to become active participants in a CME. Haughey and Anderson suggest that it is helpful to separate the technical-support responsibilities into two groups: situations where learners should contact their Internet service provider (ISP) and those where the educational institution should provide technical support. They also observed that learners were developing their technical skills through various sources such as friends, learners, libraries, news groups, and search engines.

2.6.2. Enabling Technologies
Berg (1996) saw two types of interaction in learning: interaction with the learning content and interpersonal interaction. CMC allows interaction with and about the learning content. Interaction is important in higher-order learning for analysis, synthesis, and evaluation. Well-designed instructions and expert intervention will support and improve the learning. Ferguson (2001) pointed out that

[t]ools are not teaching: tools are for teaching. Teaching will always remain the responsibility of the instructor. Knowing why you should use a tool makes the how, an easier task. No matter how good any course management software is, without the underlying pedagogy, it will be an empty tool. Good online courses do not happen; they are created. (p. 93)

Hughey and Anderson (1998) described network learning:

Network Learning happens when learners and instructors use computers to exchange information and access resources as part of a learning endeavour. The types of communication modes, content and learning activities that can be accessed through computers are growing daily as new ways are found to use computer networks to assist in teaching/learning processes. (p. 3)

Gillani and Relan (1996) noted that the introduction of frame technology has facilitated better instructional design:

The contribution of Vygotsky's social cognitive theories, impact of neuroscience findings, and appropriated instructional themes simulate a rethinking of interactive instructional design that is well suited for Web-based instructional models. However, such instructional design for the Web was not possible until frame technology was introduced with Netscape Navigator 2.0 in 1995. (p. 232)

Malikowski (1996) noted that computer conferencing helps to create an online social area and fosters social cohesion and interaction: 'Teachers experienced with online learning emphasize the importance of fostering social cohesion in an online class. A surprising level of cohesion can occur by using conferencing, as long as the opportunity for non-class-related interaction is promoted' (p. 284).

2.6.3. Design and Development in a CME

Chambers (1993) suggested that the aim of any humanities course is to teach students how to

- read a range of texts, analyse, interpret, and judge the material;
- engage with the ideas and learn to think in these terms;
- grasp the purpose, assumptions, belief systems and values underlying the debate;
- understand how arguments are constructed, what counts as evidence, and how it is used; and
- learn to speak and write within the relevant conventions.

Rossner and Stockley (1997) suggested that educational institutions are embracing CME because

- CME can provide a rich, interactive learning environment;
- internal and external pressures demand a proactive response to new technology;
- government-funding initiatives are available to support learning networks;
- government directives to increase the number of learners in response to mass education and the need to cater for a diverse groups and promoting lifelong learning by focusing on online learning has shifted focus for face to face education to online education;
- CME facilitates the provision of cost-effective, high-quality education to greater numbers of learners;
- CME are independent of time and place;
- CME can reach students in remote areas; and
- CME takes education to the learner.

The selection of the technology infrastructure should be based on appropriate teaching and learning pedagogy and should support various formats for communication, discussion, the negotiation of ideas, and collaboration. The technology should be adaptable and interactive in order to support practical simulations and modelling. Virtual learning should represent a 'reflective practicum' as a medium for interaction.

Although there are compelling reasons to invest in new technologies, decision making in this area is becoming more difficult. Bates (1997) provided a useful framework to help decision makers select technology applications: the ACTIONs (access, costs, teaching and learning, interactivity, organisation, novelty, speed). He suggests these criteria to aid selection of the most-appropriate technologies for differing contexts:

- the technologies should work in a wide variety of contexts;
- the technologies should facilitate decision making at a strategic or institution-wide level, and also at a tactical or instructional level;
- the technologies should address equally instructional and operational issues;
- it is possible to identify critical differences between technologies, thus enabling an appropriate mix of technologies to be chosen for a given context; and
- the technologies should accommodate new developments.

2.6.4. Conclusion

This literature review has traced the developments in online and distance learning, and the issues for teaching and learning that have emerged because of changes in the technology. The student experience of learner support changes with the developments in technology. Supporting learners' diverse expectations is challenging for teaching institutions because the technology is changing much faster than the infrastructure of the institutions themselves.

The early scholars and practitioners expressed doubts about whether technology could support online learners effectively; the later work shows that the opposite is true. This literature review demonstrates that, far from reducing the level of learner support, new communication technologies are actually enhancing it and stimulating some searching questions for educational institutions. I conclude that tutors need to take a structured approach to reviewing and restructuring their technology requirements in order to meet specific learner needs. They should base this activity on the organisational, social, pedagogical, and technical dimensions of learner support, placing the learners' voices at the heart of their deliberations.

ENDNOTES

1. See http://www.jisc.ac.uk/elearning_pedagogy.html.
2. See http://www.jisc.ac.uk/uploaded_documents/understanding_ mylearning.doc.
3. See Department for Education and Skills (2005), at http://www. dfes.gov.uk/publications/e-strategy/.

CHAPTER 3

RESEARCH METHODOLOGY

3.1. CHAPTER OVERVIEW

This chapter describes the research design, the conduct of the research, and evaluation. My aim in this study was to explore voices of online- and distance-learning practitioners, and to identify the effective practices in learner support in a CME. In this chapter, I describe the study setting and the learning environment. I set out my research objective, my research design, and my research questions. I discuss the rationale for the 'learner voice' as the focus of this study. I explain the boundaries to the study, the factors I considered in selecting the research and the research ethics. I describe the method of data collection, the data content, and my approach to the analysis. Finally, I discuss the interpretation and evaluation of the evidence. The outcome from this research is an understanding of how the CME has affected the students' thinking and learning processes and how these have evolved over time. This provides practitioners with insights into the factors that we can use to judge the overall success of the online-learning environment.

3.2. THE STUDY SETTING AND THE LEARNING ENVIRONMENT

3.2.1. The Study Setting

The setting for this study was the Institute of Educational Technology (IET) at the Open University. The IET provides advice on the use of communication technologies in support of teaching, particularly in e-learning and distance learning. The Open University offers a Master of Arts Degree in Open and Distance Education, which is open to postgraduate students from countries around the world, and is delivered entirely online. Students complete three 60-credit courses for the award of the M.A., and they may study the courses in any order. For this case study, I selected a 6-week block called 'Supporting Learners in ODL Systems', from the 9-month course H804, on the 'Implementation of Open and Distance Learning'.

Since the University offered course H804 internationally, this made it more difficult to elicit the learners' background, culture, and social issues, which would have an effect on the learning. Forty students were taking this course. The students were divided into three groups, each with their own tutor and learning environment. My group comprised 12 mature adult learners from different countries and from different backgrounds and professions.

One of the topics in course H804 was 'Learner experiences of learner support in a CME'. The 'learner support' theme lasted for 6 weeks. The student cohort consisted of 14 students, and the activity included contributions from a chairperson, tutor, librarian, guest speaker, technician, administrator, and students. Over the course of discussing and learning about the learner support theme, the participants exchanged around 350 messages on the eBBs.

3.2.2. The Learning Environment
The Open University delivered course H804 entirely online, which made the use of a computer compulsory. The course resources consisted of books and other printed materials (including specially written reports, articles, and overview essays); a computer conferencing facility; a Web site with links to specific online resources, and an electronic library of audio cassettes and video tapes.

The teaching and learning was based on computer conferences; the course conference area was the hub of the course. The Open University had developed the computer-mediated conferencing system eBBS. The software was a basic asynchronous system similar in function to proprietary groupware computer-conferencing systems. Tutors used a combination of media for teaching and assessment, including e-mail, conferencing, and the Internet.

The tutor time allocated for this course was 6 hours per week. Students were required to log on to the conference area three times a week, and the university expected them to study between 12 and 16 hours a week. Students worked through the activities at their own pace. They had to complete a literature search on the subject before posting their contributions to the conference area.

All students received in advance a set of reading materials related to each topic for discussion. At the end of the course block, the tutor asked students to write a report or an essay about the topic and to contribute to the discussion. Every instructor who has used online conferencing for class discussion knows that students do not regularly participate in online discussions unless the course structure requires this (Harasim, 1990). Accordingly, in this class, students' contribution to the conference area carried a 10% mark towards the assignment. Students were motivated also by feedback messages from the tutor posted to the conference area.

The course conference area facilitated asynchronous collaboration, and students used it to explore course-related issues through a series of online group activities. There was a considerable amount of online collaboration between members of each subgroup. The tutor created an appropriate climate for learning by giving the students feedback on how they were using the online-learning materials and conducting their collaborative activities.

3.2.3. Creating an Appropriate Climate
for Learning

In comparison to conventional teaching methods of 'sage on the stage', the self-paced and individualised approach places greater responsibility on the students to manage and monitor their learning. However, the success of an online-learning course depends largely upon the creation of an appropriate climate for learning within the class. Malikowski (1996) highlighted the importance of creating an online social area as one factor in fostering social cohesion and interaction: 'Teachers experienced with online learning emphasize the importance of fostering social cohesion in an online class. A surprising level of cohesion can occur by using conferencing, as long as the opportunity for non-class related interaction is promoted' (p. 284). Confidence in using the online discussion tools is another important factor. Students and tutors and should be able to express their insights honestly and openly in the knowledge that others will value their opinions. The social climate should promote critical evaluation and reflection, enabling learners to reach a better understanding of the factors that facilitate or impede their learning.

The tutor began the block by posting a topic for discussion, and provided links, reading, and resources in preparation for the online interaction. The tutor monitored and facilitated the discussion and intervened as necessary, to keep the discussion focused and meaningful. The tutor's pedagogical interactions with individuals through e-mail and discussion were designed to support the learners in these processes. All the course activities were designed to encourage dialogue and interaction, in a constructivist manner, by making participants more explicitly aware of their own cognitive and metacognitive activities through the processes of articulation, reflection, and exploration of ideas.

3.3. THE RESEARCH OBJECTIVE

Those involved in open and distance learning often take it for granted that supporting the learner in a computer-mediated environment is the same as supporting the learner in a conventional face-to-face setting. The proportion of enrolled students who continue to the end of their course is an important measure of performance for academic institutions. Inevitably, some students will drop out for various reasons; dissatisfaction with the level of support can be an important factor. The number of students who drop out of their course may correlate with the quality of learner support.

My research objective was to identify the effective practices for supporting student learning within a computer-mediated environment. My hypothesis was that we know little about the process of designing a learner-support system in real time and in a real world context. Following on Morgan's (1997) research in student learning, I aimed to present the learners' experience as the basis for 'critical reflection' on the effective practice of teaching and learning. I hoped to raise awareness among trainers, course designers, and policymakers in order to improve the quality of learning and the practice of teaching and learning.

The primary question was: How can tutors use the specific elements of a CME and other interactive technological features effectively to support a known learner or a group of learners? The aim was to allow the practitioners' voices on learner support in a CME to emerge and to highlight challenges for institutions, stakeholders, learners, and current educational cultures. The primary research question led me on to consider the evidence that would answer these subsidiary questions:

- Why is learner support important?
- What contribution does knowing one's learner make to learner support?
- How do course-design strategies affect learner support in a CME?
- What choice of media and technologies should tutors make available in a specific learner-support system?
- What makes for an effective learner support-system in a particular context?

I focused my research on students' interaction with the purpose-built CME system and selected this messaging activity within the online learner-support system for my study. I examined and analysed the students' learning experience from their messages. My goal was to develop a greater understanding of learner support in a computer-mediated environment which, in turn, should lead to more effective learner support.

3.4. THE RESEARCH DESIGN

My experience as both a practitioner and as a participant on the course influenced my approach to the research design. I based the structure of this study on the four dimensions of the e-learning framework, which I discussed in chapter 2: the organisational, the social, the pedagogical, and the technical.

When selecting a research methodology, 'it is proper to select that paradigm whose assumptions are best met by the phenomenon investigated' (Guba, 1981, p. 76). The methodology employed should be judged in terms of its success 'in investigating educational problems deemed important' (Howe & Eishenhart, 1990, p. 2).

There is an extensive literature on the respective merits of quantitative and qualitative research methods. Campbell and Stanely (1966, as cited in Howe, 2005) take an extreme position; they advocate an experimental methodology, which they describe as

> the only means of settling disputes regarding educational practice, as the only way of verifying educational improvements, and as the only way of establishing a cumulative tradition in which improvements can be introduced without the faddish discard of old wisdom in favour of inferior novelties. (p. 308)

In contrast, Guba (1992) suggested that a radical paradigm shift towards qualitative research will quite rightly (in his view) replace and eradicate quantitative methods entirely.

Sharpe et al. (2005) recommended Interpretative Phenomenological Analysis (IPA) as a suitable analytical tool for studies that explore individual experience. IPA combines two qualitative traditional research methods:

1. *Phenomenological*: capture participants' own experience.
2. *Interpretive*: the researcher enters the process of interpretation by bringing his/her own experience to bear on the reflective process of achieving meaning. Interpretation emerges from participants' accounts rather than from prior hypotheses.

In recognition of the subjective nature of the learner experience in my specific context, I decided to adopt Interpretative Phenomenological Analysis (IPA) as the most appropriate methodology for this study (Reid et al., 2005).

IPA is a relatively recent qualitative approach, developed by psychologists and now used widely by researchers in health and clinical and social psychology, particularly in the United Kingdom. IPA seeks to understand lived experiences and how participants make sense of their own experiences, rather than making prior assumptions and testing hypotheses. Most IPA work has used semistructured interviews; the methodology requires the participants to provide their own detailed narrative and to interpret their understanding of their experiences first for themselves and subsequently for the topic that they are studying (Creanor, 2006):

> IPA...rests on the premise, as does the LEX study, that the interviewee is expert on their own experience. This inductive approach deliberately avoids testing hypotheses and making prior assumptions, but rather encourages participants to provide their own detailed narrative, interpreting their understanding of their experiences firstly for themselves and subsequently for the researcher. Its aim is to capture and explore the meanings that participants assign to their own experiences, reduce the complexity of

the resultant data through rigorous analysis and provide an interpretative, transparent and reflective account of the outcome. (p. 3)

IPA provides a fuller, richer account than would be possible with quantitative methods, and it gives the researcher flexibility in probing interesting areas that emerge. Using UPA, researchers can also track practices that influence performance; analysts can use project data to identify 'best practice'. Researchers tape the interviews and transcribe them verbatim; they then carry out detailed qualitative analysis in order to elicit key themes. However, IPA involves more than a summary of the learners' voices from the messages; the interpretation involves significant input from the researcher. I considered that an interpretive, qualitative methodology was appropriate for my purpose because it was compatible with the subject, and because there is a dearth of research of this kind, on 'learners' voices'.

3.5. The Rationale for the Leaner Voice as the Focus of This Study

Entwistle (2002) commented on the difference between research and reality: 'there are crucial differences between the idealized world described by research and the actual world experienced by participants' (p. 16). This comment aroused my curiosity and prompted my decision to select the 'learner voice' as the focus for this study. The proceedings of the JISC Online Conference, 'Innovating e-Learning' (2006), noted that

> [m]any voices compete for attention in the elearning debate—teachers, developers, managers, learning technologists and ICT technicians. The learners' voices can be pretty hard to hear in this general hubbub. Too often circumstances conspire to prevent those who hear them

> best—their teachers—from sharing their knowledge with each other. (p. 15)

My starting point was the premise that learners are experts on their own experience; they can share, modify, and enrich this experience, to illuminate best practice in learner support strategies in a CME employing the four dimensions: organisation, pedagogical, social, and technical strategies.

Mayes (2006) suggested that research in e-learning has neglected the learner perspective:

> Thus, most research has been devoted to exploring the effect of differences in learning environments, pedagogical procedures or learning materials on learning outcomes. This mainstream approach reveals some influence of constructivist pedagogy, but largely neglects a genuinely learner-centred perspective: that students experience formal learning in emotional terms, that their motivation to learn is only understandable by looking at their lives holistically, and that technology is embedded in their social experience. (p. 3)

He suggests a methodology that can display naturalistic and contextual characteristics in order to fill two gaps that he identified in data collection methodologies:

1. stories or narrative to capture the diverse ways in which students use technology, and
2. attempts to elicit beliefs and intentions.

Sharpe et al. (2005) supported the holistic view in which learners talk about what matters to them:

> A holistic view of e-learning should lead to a methodology which is open ended and empowering enough

to allow the learners to be the ones who highlight the issues which are important to them...We noted that the majority of the research to date has focused on observable learner behaviors. There is an opportunity to design the forthcoming research study so that it is able to shed light on the learner intentions and rationales behind commonly noted observable behaviors. (p. 4)

The methodology I used in this study also maps closely to that proposed by Mayes (2006), which he termed 'interview plus'—where the 'plus' represents chosen artefacts or activities. Some of the artefacts I identified in this study are

- the learners' own messages that they contributed to the conference area,
- the learners' work space represented as 'file area',
- administrator's e-mail messages,
- technician's e-mail and conference messages,
- messages posted by guest speakers 'Ask and Expert',
- messages posted by lurkers from other class group, and
- messages posted by the group tutor and by tutors from other class groups.

I used a 'three zones' approach for analysis, comprising inputs (antecedents), process (conversation), and outputs (outcomes). These zones represent artefacts chosen to aid the learners' voices and provide an orderly way to think about learner support in a CME. My approach concurs with that advocated by Sharpe et al. (2005), which emphasises learners' experience and perceptions rather than interviews or surveys. It should be simple and easy for others to follow, understand, and adapt for themselves.

3.6. FACTORS CONSIDERED IN SETTING UP THIS STUDY

3.6.1. Factors Relating to the Open University

The main factors that I considered when selecting the Open University for this study were:

a. the Open University's reputation as an international provider of open and distance education and its academic integrity, and
b. the quality of research in the Institute of Educational Technology and its contribution to the development of online teaching and learning.

The Institute of Educational Technology (IET) is a centre of international excellence in research and development of online, open and distance learning. Academic integrity is very important in the context of open and distance learning.

The discursive nature of CMC, with messages in the conference area open to scrutiny by others, meant that students were aware of representing others' work fairly in the context of their own. It was the tutor's responsibility to ensure that students:

*   reflected critically on the issues raised in the course,
*   considered a range of points of view from their peers on the course,
*   developed their own views,
*   stated the argument clearly with supporting evidence and proper referencing of sources, and
*   drew on their own experience.

3.6.2. Factors Relating to the Qualities of the Tutor

The qualities of the tutor are critical to the provision of effective learner support in a CME. The teaching and learning process is an interaction between teacher and student to create the conversational framework for academic learning. Teaching that incorporates discussions reflects the iterative character of the learning process (Laurillard, 2002). I considered that enthusiasm and approachability, organisational skills, ability to give direction and feedback, familiarity with the learning environment and course materials, and confidence in using the online tools combine to determine his/her effectiveness. These factors influence the tutor's ability to scaffold the learning and build up the students' skills and knowledge (Vygotsky, 1978). The online messages from the tutor for course H804 demonstrated considerable skills in generating ideas and in facilitating the discussions in the conference area. This factor influenced my decision to select this particular online course for my study of learner support.

3.6.3. Factors for Selecting the Student Cohort

The participants in this research project were mature students on the M.A. course in Open and Distance Education at the Open University in the United Kingdom.

The course aim was to help students to develop as reflective practitioners in open and distance education. The course content was grounded in the real concerns, practices, and approaches of practitioners, and used theory and research to illuminate the practice.

I selected a cohort of 14 students from the forty students on course H804. The group consisted of 11 male and 4 female students, all of whom had previous experience of formal online education. Most of the cohort came from the education profession; they knew what they were looking for from this course. The group was subdivided into two smaller groups in the virtual environment, one consisting of two females and six males, and a second group consisting of one female and five males.

The tutor and the students were familiar with the constructivist approach employed in course H804, and they understood the value of collaborative discussion with their peers online. The students in the H804 cohort already knew one another and the tutor, as most of them were continuing from courses H801 and H802.

3.6.4. Factors Related to the Researcher

I have 15 years of experience in face-to-face learner support, and 8 years of experience in online learner support, which includes face-to-face and online teaching, curriculum development, the design and development of online courses, and tutoring online. The experience I have gained since completing the Open University programme, and the increasing amount of attention surrounding the issue of online learner support, has prompted me to consider this an important issue in the field of education.

My role in this research does not fit the conventional mode of the 'insider researcher' (the tutor researching into his or her own practice) or the 'outsider researcher' (the researcher approaching a situation in which he/she has had no previous involvement). When I studied course H804, I did not anticipate carrying out research on online learner support. I was simply a fellow student at that time, a peer to the other students, engaging in knowledge sharing and the exchange of ideas. To the tutor, I was a student with the goal of achieving further quality of learning. I conducted this research several years after completing the course, and therefore 'researcher intervention' and bias was not an issue. I would now describe my role as that of a 'detached outsider researcher' who was part of the social situation.

3.7. BOUNDARIES

In order to focus this study on practitioners' voices and keep the research to manageable proportions, I set these boundaries:

- I selected one, 14-week discussion period in course H804, in which the students were discussing 'Learner support in Open and Distance Learning'.
- I selected a cohort of 14 students studying the course, most of whom had studied courses H801 and H802 previously, and who were therefore familiar with the online-learning environment.
- The student cohort comprised students who were experienced in theories and practices of Open and Distance Education.

3.8. RESEARCH ETHICS

Sound research ethics demands that people have the right to make an informed choice about their participation in research, and to decide to what extent they are willing to participate. Three Canadian federal granting councils have issued guidelines on ethical research. Failure to secure individuals' permission can mean that a funded study cannot take place (Rourke, Anderson, Garrison, & Archer, 2001). The Council of the British Educational Research Association (BERA, 2004) also provides detailed ethical guidelines, which help the researcher to consider all the aspects of conducting educational research in a given context.

A problem with studying messages is that participants may be unwilling to make their messages available to the researcher because they may contain private information. Rourke et al. (2001) suggested two possible solutions:

- each participant could sign a release form, which explains the nature of the research, the potential outcomes, and other matters of concern, or
- the researcher can strip out all personal details from all the messages, including log-in names and e-mail addresses.

Rourke et al. recognised that there is no easy solution to gaining consent; researchers must either expend time and energy to obtain it or strip the personal identification out of interview/message transcripts.

In this particular research project, it was not feasible to gain individual students' written consent to the research because it was difficult to obtain the course participants' postal addresses. As an alternative, I used e-mail as an informal means of gaining consent. My e-mail explained the nature and purpose of my research and asked students whether they would have any concerns about my using their message contributions to the conference area. I also requested permission from the chairperson at the Institute of Educational Technology and from the course tutor. Because I was a student on the course and knew all the participants, gaining consent proved easy.

3.9. DATA COLLECTION AND ANALYSIS

3.9.1. Content Analysis

I carried out this research a few years after completing course H804. It was not feasible to use interviews or surveys at this point; what was available to me was the archive of messages captured during the course. The question of representative sampling was not relevant. My research focused on the entire archive of messages generated from the 6-week discussion in the conference area.

The 'Learner support' Block focused around a particular theme in online education. Tutors, practitioners, a study guide, reading material, guests, and speakers were organised in advance, in preparation for the course activities. During the activity, participants posted messages to the discussion group in response to the tutor's topic. Meanings from messages formed the central discourse and influenced those associated with it. I used content analysis as the technique to study the learners' messages posted to the eBBs conference area. Berelson (1953) defined content analysis as 'a research technique for the objective, systematic, and quantitative description of manifest content of communications' (p. 18).

Content analysis is a methodology that has great potential, although it is difficult and time consuming (Rourke et al., 2001); it focuses on the actual content and internal features of media. Researchers use content analysis to determine the presence of certain words, concepts, themes, characters, phrases, patterns, or sentences within texts or set of texts and to quantify this presence in an objective manner. They do so by coding and breaking down the text into manageable categories, at various levels. Mason (1991b) called on researchers to take up the challenge of content analysis both as a key to professionalism in the field and for the educational value of the activity. Researchers can judge the reliability of content analysis in terms of its stability, accuracy, reproducibility, the consistency of the coding and the classification of categories. The validity of content analysis can be judged by comparing the correspondence of the categories to the conclusions, and the generalisability of results to the theory.

Within this study, I wanted to bring out how learners perceive a learner-support system. The term 'learner support' can mean different things to different people. A few students may feel that requesting support is a sign of weakness; others may see offers of support as an interruption to their studies rather than a positive intervention. Some students will see learner support as a positive means of seeking positive reinforcement for their learning. I developed an analytic framework to study the processes that affect learner support in a computer-mediated environment. I based this on the conversational framework developed by Laurillard (1993) and Rourke et al. (2001), which represented the most current thinking on the integration of constructivist learning and critical thinking. I captured the learners' comments, discussion, and responses from different media postings, using Laurillard's conversational framework to transform the transcripts into useable information.

The conversational model has two aspects: the first relates to the technological tools and features that are used in the CME; the second relates to the learning processes that students engaged in, making meaning of their learning. One of the characteristics of this model is the way in which students and tutor interact. An examination of the 350 messages collected during the H804 study block showed that the primary purpose of the research on learner support was to

- acquire new knowledge on how academic research is carried out;
- improve institution policies and procedures on embedding technology with teaching and learning;
- improve student performance;
- highlight social, organisational, and pedagogical issues in teaching online;
- understand students' needs better in order to give more appropriate guidance and counselling.

I read the messages that the participants posted to the conference area and considered how the technology supported these interactions. I determined the content validity of the messages by my own judgment of each message. I then posted the messages to a database under one of four different fields:

- discursive,
- adaptive,
- interactive, and
- reflective.

For example, I looked at messages where the tutor supported the processes whereby the students discussed and reflected upon their learning (discursive), and where the tutor had summarised and revised what learning had taken place (adaptive), and posted these messages to the corresponding fields in the database.

Content analysis asks questions of the text and seeks answers from it. The work of Marton and Saljo (1984) is a useful guide on interaction with text. The participants' written contributions in the conference area proved to be a fruitful source from which to develop my understanding of learner support in online and distance education. I analysed the content of the online communications qualitatively and enumerated the evidence of collaboration and learner support. I brought out insights and reflections from different perspectives and mapped them to models of online learner support. Individual messages and the pooling of different experiences provided either a challenge or a confirmation to commonly held theories and practices. It is through this critical process of examining assumptions and ways of thinking and acting that a framework can be constructed to narrow the gap in our understanding of learner support.

3.9.2. The Unit of Analysis

The unit of analysis was an individual post. I treated each post as a separate unit, regardless of by whom it was posted. (I made an exception for deleted posts and posts repeated in error.) Each message comprised the variables seen in table 1.

I saved all the messages from the subgroup of course H804 course into an html archive format. I used Microsoft Access to define the variables, transferred all messages to the database, and placed the variables in appropriate fields. I then transferred the messages to a Microsoft Word document and coded the messages according to the experts' definitions.

TABLE 1. Variables.

Variables	Explanation
Name	Message originator
Emoticon	A small graphic reflects the intention of the message
Date	A date stamp when the message been sent
Message number	A tag gives the message number
Thread subject	The message header
Thread depth	The depth of the thread within a topic
Comment	The content of the message
Activity	Activity number

TABLE 2. Framework zones.

Antecedents Zone	Conversation Zone	Outcomes Zone
Organisation	Discursive	Assignments
Technology	Adaptive	Activities
Task structure	Interactive	
Group structure	Reflective	
Administration		
Learner profile		
Technical		

I analysed and mapped the messages according to the framework zones: antecedent, conversation, and outcome. The three zones are a distillation of the research questions mentioned in chapter 3, which focus on the areas that illuminate our understanding of learner support in a CME.

The participants expressed their messages on learner-support systems in terms of theory and their personal experience. I read each message several times in order to ensure that I had interpreted it accurately. Interpretation, transparency, and plausibility are important features in understanding individuals' experiences (Creanor, 2006). Any message may contain many assertions; my study looked for the central purpose of the whole message, and at how it fitted with the three zones: antecedent, conversation, and outcome.

The message portion of any posting consisted only of the participant's contribution to the discussion, as seen in the body of the message. I did not consider hyperlinks to external material or the information line of the message, although this information was useful as context to help interpret the message. I used two methods of data interpretation:

- I read each message and then assigned it to one of the framework categories.
- I queried the database using Microsoft Access query commands.

3.10. REVIEW AND DISCUSSION

3.10.1. Research Design and Comparison

In this review and discussion, I focus on these issues: the research design and comparison with other research designs; factors affecting the interpretation of data; and generalisations from the evidence in this study. There is little rigorous, empirical data that explores the effect of CMC on learner support. By focusing on how learners are supported in a computer-mediated environment, this study sought to capture students' emerging understanding of learner support in a computer-mediated environment while they studied the topic. Parlett and Dearden (1977) noted that

> the researcher is concerned to familiarise himself thoroughly with the day to day setting or settings he is studying...he makes no attempt to manipulate, control, or eliminate situational variables but takes as given the complex scene he encounters. His chief task is to unravel it, isolate its significant features; delineate cycles of cause and effect; and comprehend relationships between beliefs and practices. (p. 10)

Hammersley (1993) suggested that the major issue in the differentiation of methodologies is a matter of case selection. The research approach has two differentiating features. It involves (as in this study) a small number of learners who are characterised by certain behaviours and qualities, which occur naturally rather than being created by the researcher.

Kaplan and Maxwell (1994) contended that the understanding of a phenomenon from the participants' point of view and from the particular social and institutional context is largely lost when researchers quantify textual data. I chose to carry out an interpretive study rather than comparative-, experimental-, or survey-based research, because this was the most appropriate methodology for the research questions I wished to answer.

3.10.2. Interpreting the Data

Online discussion provides an excellent vehicle for online learning because there is greater time for reflection, more democratic participation, and the benefits of improving writing skills where learners post messages to the conference area regardless of time and place (Benbunan-Fich & Hiltz, 1999). There are two criteria for evaluating the success of online learner support for this study class, which need to be considered jointly. The first relates to the intrinsic quality of the teaching, and the second to how well the students used the discussion tools for knowledge construction.

It was not feasible to evaluate learning outcomes from students' assignments, as I did not have access to them. However, I was able to judge learning outcomes from five sources:

- the extent and quality of contribution the conference area;
- the appropriate use of resources: course books, other books or articles, and the online discussions;
- the quality of the students' insights into the distinctive features of his/her own ODL context and the appropriateness of proposed action;
- the clarity and coherence of the written argument or discourse; and
- the appropriateness of the presentations, for example, style, grammar, spelling, paragraphing, and referencing.

Three issues affected the interpretation of the data:

- The difficulty of establishing that messages posted to the conference area were posted by those who meant to post them. (I ignored duplicate messages and deleted messages).
- It was not feasible to analyse the reference hyperlinks to external Web sites.
- It was not feasible to analyse links to e-mails sent from the conference area, and therefore the main focus of my research was the text messages posted to the conference area.

3.10.3. Generalising From the Findings
of This Study

This study focused on an issue of particular interest, using only a small number of participants. We cannot assume that that another researcher could replicate this study precisely (Yin, 1993), as the student cohort was not a representative sample from which one can extrapolate general principles for a wider population. However, Hamel et al. (1993) suggested that the literature provides some insight into acceptance of an entity that can form a part of the global concentration. Smith and Osborne (2003) have noted the benefits of generalisation from a theoretical perspective in this type of study. '[T]he links are made between a particular IPA study, the professional judgment of users of the study, and the wider literature' (p. 39).

Mayes (2006) contended that a small size sample implies a more detailed account of the participants' experience:

> The aim is to give as detailed an account as possible of the meaning to the participants of their own experiences, and this is a very resource-intensive process...

> It is normal for IPA studies to finish with general claims, but it is important that generalisations do not emerge too early in the analysis. The purposive sampling favoured by IPA should mean that the participants form a homogeneous group with reference to the research questions. This requirement will often be in conflict with the need to be inclusive of other attributes (such as gender or social class, say).

> IPA is not an appropriate methodology for comparative analysis (e.g. comparing subsets of participants). The main requirement is that participants are 'living' the key issue, and they have the required 'expertise' to talk about it. (p. 7)

Experienced practitioners should be able to assess the significance of these study findings for their own teaching and learning.

CHAPTER 4

RESEARCH FINDINGS FROM THE STUDY CLASS

4.1. CHAPTER OVERVIEW

In this chapter, I present my research on the study class. I analyse the findings qualitatively, relating them to the evaluation framework outlined in the previous chapter. I have drawn the evidence principally from the online environment of course H804. This includes the course administration, conferencing, assessment server, filearea (the online student workspace), and the course resources. In section 4.2, I examine evidence from the Antecedents Zone to provide an overview of preparing students for online learning. I use evidence from the messages selectively to demonstrate the relevance of this zone in learner support.

TABLE 3. The Antecedents Zone.

The Antecedents Zone
Organisation
Technology
Task structure
Group structure
Administration
Learner profile
Technical

TABLE 4. The Conversation Zone.

The Conversation Zone	
Discursive	• The teacher and student make ideas available to each other • The teacher and student agree on learning goals • The teacher provides an environment in which learners can interact
Adaptive	• The teacher is responsible for using the relationship between his/her own and the students' ideas to determine the focus of the continuing dialogue
Interactive	• The students act to achieve the task goal • The teacher provides meaningful feedback on the actions that relate to the goal or task.
Reflective	• The teacher has clearly defined goals for learner to achieve. • The teacher must support the process in which students link the feedback on their actions to the topic goal for every level of description with the topic structure.

TABLE 5. The Outcomes Zone.

The Outcomes Zone
Assignments
Activities

In section 4.3, I examine the evidence from the Conversation Zone to provide an overview of the online tools available to facilitate dialogue and the exchange of ideas. I also look at the structuring for each interaction, for example, linking students' e-mail within the software. For any learning activity in the conversational framework, we should consider how well the tools provide for dialogue and for structuring conversations. The course designer should be able to construct learning activities to suit the ideas in the learning goal for each topic. I have used Laurillard's conversational framework to report my findings (Laurillard, 1993), as seen in table 4.

In section 4.4, I present my findings on the Outcomes Zone, which is where participants present and exchange their ideas (see table 5).

4.2 THE ANTECEDENTS ZONE

4.2.1. The Organisation

Supporting learners' diverse expectations presents challenges to teaching institutions because the technology is changing faster and responding more flexibly than the infrastructure of the institutions. In order to support various forms of communication, discussion, negotiation of ideas, and collaboration, course designers should base the technology infrastructure on the appropriate teaching and learning pedagogy. The design team members for course H804 were aware of these issues and considered access, administration, ease of navigation, and the human support requirements thoroughly; they responded well to the learners' needs. The 'Welcome to the Open University' booklet provides a useful way of introducing the learning methods and outcomes.

Three key elements—identity, interaction, and time/duration— provide a starting point to learner support (Thorpe, 2001). Knowing the learners' identities is what distinguishes 'learner support' from other elements of Open and Distance Education systems. The process of interacting synchronously or asynchronously with a learner or group of learners who know one another happens in two contexts—the institutional and course contexts. 'Learners need support with regard to their operation with both' of the following:

a. institutional systems (such as knowing what is on offer, how to apply, how to claim a refund, make a payment, choose a course, etc.) before, during, and after course study; and

b. the course they are studying, such as how best to complete a particular assignment, how to contact and work with other students on the course, how to make sense of something in the course material, whether their contributions to the course conference are relevant, well conceived or otherwise, and so on. It is this area, particularly CMC and the Web, that are challenging our concept of learner support.

Learner support is essentially about roles, structures, and environments—therefore, support roles and supportive people, together with support structures and supportive environments'. (p. 3)

However, Thorpe's view of the institutional systems does not go deep enough to reflect the effort required to develop a successful learner-support system. Designers need to base many of the early decisions about the type, context, and scale of online support on an analysis of the prospective learners' needs. The more information we are able to gather, the better informed the decision making will be. Planning support services to meet learners' diverse needs can be challenging, but this is a vital element in enhancing the quality of teaching and learning.

The teaching approach in Course H804 emphasises collaboration between students and online contributions. It implies that all academic support services are available online. The University makes the course material available in digital format, and the teaching model is resource-based learning and group work, coached and guided by a tutor. From the outset, the amount of money available and how institutions use these funds affect the design and delivery of learner support. Sometimes government intervention dictates the resources available, and political will influences the provision. Regardless of whether the institution provides support through the 'Passchendaele model' or a 'Lone Ranger and Tonto' approach, without sufficient funding to enable tutors to select the right hardware and software, the outcome is less likely be effective. Selecting the right hardware and software requires careful planning and skilled decision making (Romiszowski, 1997). 'The undisputed technical advantages of making information more easily and more democratically available are to some extent undermined by human skill limitations on effectively using such as information network' (p. 32).

Coordination is important (Rossner & Stockley, 1997) in order to create the technological vision for learner support at the organisational, technical, social, and pedagogical level. The course team for H804 captured their design ideas in detailed specifications. They evaluated learner support using student feedback, tutor feedback, pilots involving learners, and a course team review.

Learning Contracts

A learning contract is important to the learning outcomes (Hudspeth, 1996, as cited in Khan, 1997):

> Multiple reasons exist for moving to new means and methods of assessing learner outcomes in an Internet environment. The highly interactive nature of the medium, the volatility and currency of information, remote access of instruction and instructional resources—these and many other reasons suggest that new and innovative approaches are needed. Within the context of effective testing, both to provide feedback to the learner and in terms of judging achievement, a learning contract is recommended. (p. 356)

Many messages on the eBBS concerned learner support. Student4 (msg#10) emphasises the importance of the institution's commitment and the benefit of a learner contract in clarifying expectations:

> From this experience of mine I have learnt that it is extremely important in DE (and certainly in other modes) to clarify the framework, principles and resources related to collective and individual student support on the one hand, and the students' commitments on the other. Hence a sort of more or less formal contract of mutual obligations may be established and function as an important

guidance for all parts throughout the course. (From the other side of the table I have experienced that almost every course has one or more students with enormous (and unrealistic in terms of resources) expectations of all kinds of support from the educational institution. (message posted May 15, 2000)

Student2 (msg#13) suggested that a learner-support system is a dynamic process and that following guidelines might shift the focus of the learning from 'student centred' to 'institution centred'. Student4 (msg#30), in response to Student8 (msg#25 'Learning to ask') said the following:

I think that I think that explicit signals/messages/ statements from the educational institution communicating that asking for support is a legal, integrated and important part of the agreed-upon educational framework and learning environment, may encourage learners to ask for support. Whether they (we) start asking for support when we feel that we need it, will depend on several circumstances:

1. The degree to which 'the course' (=all engaged) succeed in creating a secure and supportive learning environment.
2. How 'complete' the learner feels that her/his need for support is. What I try to say, is that the lesser control you (=I) feel you (=I) have, the higher the mental threshold to ask for support/help usually will be.
3. What sort of support we ask for. It is dramatically more difficult to ask a peer student to explain a subject issue (that I believe everybody else understands) or tell that I have just collapsed, than to ask for help to find a relevant reference or article on a specific topic. (message posted May 20, 2000)

The institution plays an important role in learner support (Robinson, 1995). Mark (msg#36) draws on Robinson's work when he said the following:

> Top of here list is Learner-Institution contact, that's a major theme running through our postings, so are we confirming/validating that item on her list through our postings?

> Further down the list is contact between support staff and other learners, again this is seen as important from our postings.

> Finally, the list notes that personal circumstances and lack of time are the most common reasons for dropping out. I think we can all support that finding. (message posted May 20, 2000)

Institutional Requirements for Learner Support

Student1 (msg#213) summarises reflections on the role that the institution plays in learner support, quoting the list of requirements from Rossner and Stockley (1997) chapter 41:

> 'Institutional Perspectives on Organising and Delivering Web-Based Instruction':

> • support from senior admin levels;
> • campus wide IT backbone to access Web-based instruction;
> • current library facilities need to be put online;
> • student registration via the Web;
> • access to any campus based server containing relevant info by student/faculty;
> • supporting research in hardware, software, modes of instruction;
> • input from existing faculty/technical people with tech knowledge;

- developing support systems to provide training in the educational uses of interactive technologies;
- providing on-going tech and pedagogical support to both faculty and students; and
- committing an adequate budget

The evidence from this study shows that the Open University has demonstrated commitment to its distance students. There was a sufficient infrastructure, appropriate staffing, technical support, and course administration in place. The University clearly communicated information about student services and processes of programme design and programme coordination.

4.2.2. Technology
Technology makes distance learning and open education possible; it has a substantial influence on teaching and learning, and particularly on the interaction between teachers and students, and on how they create discussions.

Design and Learner Interaction
Design is particularly important in the online-learning environment; diverse media formats allow a choice of interaction. However, Galegher and Kraut (1989) noted that

> the history of experience with telecommunications and computer-based information systems contains many instances of expensive technological failures that are at least partly attributable to designs that do not mesh well with the social and behavioural systems in which they are to be used. (p. 489)

A useful way of analysing the effectiveness of technology in the educational setting is to consider how well the media tools foster interaction.

Because there are no underpinning theories on using technologies in education, some practitioners have tried to create frameworks for classifying media effects and matching them with teaching and learning. Collis (1993) suggested these criteria for a 'potential effectiveness inventory' for the media used in distance education:

- the degree of time and place independence facilitated by the media,
- the level of realism in the instructional materials supported by the media,
- flexibility in communication paths maintained through the media;
- ease of use of the media, and
- immediacy—how fast information and feedback are available with a particular medium.

Collis also noted that

> [t]he technical attributes of the instrumentation used in distance education coupled with the instructional design decisions made with respect to the construction of this instrumentation can be evaluated with respect to these criteria and thus can offer designers more critical insights into the potential use and impact of their products. (p. 268)

I evaluated the technical design of course H804 against Collis' criteria in the following paragraphs.

Time and Place Independence
The Internet made the time and place independence possible on course H804.

Practical Instructions

The learning design of the course was based on embedding tasks into the course content, and on the connection and interaction between the participants and the material. Interaction depends on relationships—relationships to the material, the instructor, the student, and other learners. The Web pages for this course were well structured and informed students about the different paths that they could follow to achieve their learning goals. The extent of connectivity between the participants determined how they constructed the knowledge between them.

Flexibility in Communication

Four kinds of interaction were possible on course H804. With one-way interaction, the student is passive, like someone watching a film, listening to a lecture or presentation, reading Web pages, or reading a book. Most Web pages are one-way communication. The shift to interactivity occurs with advances in software development, for example, when the tutors posted a multimedia CD-ROM to students and asked them to install it on their machine and evaluate it.

Two-way, one-to-one interaction occurs when a student interacts with the tutor through letters or e-mail. Course H804 used e-mail to deal with administrative problems such as passwords and schedules for server down time. One-to-many interactions occur where the user posts a message to many people and is able to see other messages. This mode was not part of the H804 virtual learning system; students were directed to external links that hosted list-servers. Many-to-many interaction is very popular in education circles because it facilitates the highest degree of interaction and allows the user to get involved in a discussion with others. It can involve students, tutors, experts, materials, and resources in the process of constructing knowledge.

The eBBS system used in course H804 is an example of this type of interaction.

The pedagogy of a course determines the choice of technology—the emphasis should be on *how* the course uses technology, rather than simply *what* technology it uses. In contrast to the majority of Open University courses, the largest portion of course H804 used digital text, together with a printed study guide and other supplementary materials. Course H804 is an example of sound pedagogy, in that it implemented simple technology effectively—such as the eBBS online discussion forum, which used nothing more complicated than linked Web pages. However, some students experienced basic hardware and software problems.

Ease of Use

Course H804 relied entirely on telecommunication-based technologies. As a prerequisite for the course, students needed to have appropriate hardware and software and an Internet connection. The Open University course team had specified IBM-compatible hardware and software for the M.A. in Open and Distance Education, including

- a colour screen monitor,
- a Microsoft mouse and Windows-compatible printer,
- 15 MB hard-disk space or more,
- 16 MB of memory,
- a minimum central processing unit speed of 486,
- a CD-ROM drive with a certain specification,
- access to the Internet and the World Wide Web, and
- a standard word-processing package for preparing notes and assignments.

These criteria reflect the University's policy of using relatively cheap, accessible, and easy-to-use media.

Although the technical specification was clear, it had some obvious shortcomings:

- Most students have Internet Explorer instead of Netscape Navigator.
- The jargon in the specification is not easy for nontechnical users to understand.
- There is no online help to deal with hardware, software, and internet connection problems.
- Some students used a completely different system, which was not compatible with the Open University requirements.

There was an assumption that the student already owned an IBM-compatible PC or was going to buy one specifically for the course, but this failed to recognise that some students might have been using a different system already, such as the Apple Mac. Most students would use Microsoft Word to type their assignments, but different versions caused incompatibility problems.

The student was responsible for setting up the connection to the Open University's computers. The Open University advises students to seek information on hardware, software, and their Internet connection from local vendors. The course information for H804 did not mention the cost of the Internet connection, or who would bear this cost, or the cost of any changes in hardware or software. It did not explain what would happen in the event of a software crash or an equipment malfunction. Some students were unable to access certain Web pages because their browsers were not compatible with the University's software.

The test is whether the students find it easy to access the learning site and to find their way around within the learning package. Although the eBBS suffered some technical glitches during the course, in general, the system was easy to use and operate.

However, what is easy for one person may be difficult for someone else. Student3 (msg#28) describes the difficulties one her students encountered when trying to access an online course:

> My own example of learner (and tutor) support comes from T171 (You, Your Computer and the Internet). In this course, tutors welcome participants with a letter and then meet the group face to face before the course begins. A certain proportion of tutor time is given to telephone support.

> One of my group, a retired teacher, is not yet online for the May presentation. She has phoned ACS so often they say, 'Oh yes, A. Most of us here have spoken to her'. She has phoned me maybe just as often and I have talked her through installation of her disks and accessing the course Website and First Class many, many times.

> She has returned her first OU computer 'because it didn't work'. She has replacement CD-ROMs. At times, she is close to tears and at pains to tell me that she is well respected by her former students. 'But what am I doing wrong, here, Student3?' is her familiar cry. 'It doesn't work'.

> She has written both to ACS and to me. I have logged on with her user id and password with no problem. She tried again but changed her password. Then she phoned again. 'It doesn't work'. Sure enough, when I tried both her OU password and the new one, authorisation failed. This time I contacted ACS who are issuing her a new password. (message posted May 19, 2000)

Student2 (msg#31) shares Student3's concern about the technology and gives an example of the problems that distance learners face:

> I think it is a serious issue that needs to be addressed and researched. Putting courses on the web with excellent

online support system is not enough. The medium is not transparent yet and it is not easy to use. Sometimes the problem can't be solved even with human presence. The OU carried a pilot study by issuing students with mobile phones and remote software where problems can be fixed remotely. Although this approach was expensive, it did help in some area, but created problems in other areas, such as mobile phones lost, or get damaged. (message posted June 22, 2000)

The experiences of Student3 and Student2 suggest that Collis' criteria are insufficient. Course designers need to consider the technology specification and structure from the end user's perspective as well as the organisational perspective; they need to ask, 'How best can the University support students in using a complex technology that also depends upon human elements?' (msg#319). Institutions also need to consider the support costs involved in embarking on new technologies.

Immediacy and Feedback
Tutors used e-mail and the conference area to provide feedback within course H804. Students submitted their assignments electronically through the TMA assessment server, and tutors marked them and returned them through the server. The expected turnaround time for feedback on assignments was two weeks from the date of submission, and normally students would receive the feedback before the start of a new block. The course chairperson intervened if there were any delays. A postassignment area was set up within the conference area, where students could reflect and share their views. The messages contributed to the conference area contained nine references to feedback; most of these concerned the relevance and effectiveness of the feedback, particularly on Tutor Marked Assignments.

The benefit of CMC to the students lies in the immediacy of contact for queries or feedback. E-mail helped students to contact administration or their tutors with any queries, and students used the conference system for both course contribution and social interaction. However, the ease of contact could not guarantee that recipients would respond immediately.

4.2.3. The Task Structure

The online environment should be capable of supporting tasks that allow the participants to construct knowledge through discussion and interaction with learning peers and experts.

Collaborative and group learning was at the core of course H804. The eBBS software was particularly appropriate for collaborative learning and group work, as it provided the course team with suitable tools to modify, rename, add hyperlinks to, edit, and delete messages. The task activity had a different font size and colour from other messages, and messages posted to the conference area were displayed below the topic in a hierarchical manner, which was easy to see and access.

Course H804 used the FTP (File Transfer Protocol), which supports uploading and downloading different file formats, including text, audio, graphics, and video. Each student had a file area, which they accessed through the Internet browser of FTP application software. Tutors gave students a set of instructions and asked then to work together on an academic task. Students typed their messages into a text window and could preview their messages before submission; they also had the option of posting their messages in hypertext markup language (HTML) format.

The file area was hierarchically structured, and it served as a workspace for students' own work; students accessed this area from a hyperlink in the discussion area. Students used the file area in various ways; they could upload multiple documents in different formats to the file area or they could drag and drop files from their desktop and hyperlink between the file area and the conference area. They could post multiple web pages—including graphics, animation, and video and audio clips—to the file area, although this was not possible *through* the conference area, as the eBBS did not support video or audio formats.

The task structure included the creation of tasks and hyper-links to various paths and directions—links to resources, to the library, and to a plenary area where learners worked on the task aims and objectives. For example, the tutor created six threads for discussions in Block three, which related to three activities; there were two threads for the assignment and one thread for 'announcements and any general Block 3 issues or questions you want to raise'. These threads provided the boundaries within which the discussions took place.

However, the online delivery system for course H804 did not offer an integrated e-mail facility. Students were free to use whatever e-mail system they preferred; this had implications for the learner and the administrator. From the administrative perspective, this meant less policing, administration, and mod-eration. On the other hand, students may change their e-mail addresses for various reasons, and unless they inform the course administrators and tutors, it becomes impossible for the staff to maintain e-mail contact with them. From the student perspec-tive, having an e-mail address that is not generic meant that if they tried to access the course from a different machine, they were unable to read their e-mail without a complex configura-tion of the machine they were currently using. Group tasks in course H804 required the students to use e-mail, but since the eBBS did not have an integrated e-mail system, the participants had to shuttle between their external e-mail and the eBBS in order to contribute. I favour an integrated e-mail system within a learning environment because of the following:

- Learners waste time shuttling between two systems—the eBBS and the external mail system.
- An integrated e-mail system reduces the need for changes in e-mail addresses and makes the exchange of information more manageable.
- All e-mail messages are saved on the central server, which may represent good value for researchers and developers.
- An integrated e-mail system should give students a sense of belonging to the academic discipline, help to shape message contents, and reduce padding. On the other hand, it might deter students from posting messages because their personal contact details will be shared with people they do not know.
- Learners will be able to refer to one central location for technical help and advice.
- Tutor and students will have a standard e-mail address domain name, for example, a@open.uk, b@open.uk. This might be useful for classifying learners with a course, group, and location.

4.2.4. Group Structure
The two-way communication between teacher and learner is an important aspect of collaboration in a computer-mediated environment. Communication in course H804 was solely through e-mail and the eBBS conferencing system; audio and video conferencing was not available because of difficulties with bandwidth within the eBBS. The majority of the H804 course material was in digital format, whereas material for course H802 comprised a printed study guide, sets of examination papers, reading

material, media broadcast booklet, audiocassette, videocassette, and TV programmes.

Roles and Tasks

The main tool for creating the group task was the eBBS conference area. The tutor initiated the group activity (msg#0): 'The main online task in this Block (Activity 2) is a collaborative group one' (message posted May 11, 2000). The tutor posted the activity for the group to tackle and divided the group into two smaller groups. The size of a student group is important to the successful completion of the task when the prime form of interaction is the conference area of a shared document. Student2 (msg#157) suggested these roles, based on his experience in course H802: Proposer, Opposer, Researcher, Moderator, Documentalist, and Commenter.

The roles and associated tasks for each Activity were as follows:

- The Proposer of the motion posted a short message (about one screen in length) into the group conference area, amplified the proposition, and made a case for it in such a way as to encourage comment from other group members.
- The Opposer's role was to counter the Proposer's message by inputting in a message of similar length arguing from a differing point of view, and again, framed in such a way as to encourage further comment.
- The Moderator's role was to set the scene for the discussion, to encourage initial comments on the Proposer's and Opposer's messages, to encourage 'lurkers' to contribute, to keep the discussion on track, and to weave links among the different contributors' messages.

- The Documentalist's role was to summarise one or more of the set readings for the topic, pick out points relevant to the proposition, and contribute the summary to the discussion thread.
- The Researcher's role was to find other relevant readings and resources from the Web and from the set books and bring them to the attention of the group. (Collis, 1993; Khan, 1997).
- The Rapporteur's role was to prepare a summary of the overall debate (two or three screens long) and upload it into the group area on the eBBS to allow the whole group to comment before preparing a final version to go into the main Activity2 thread.
- The Commenter's role was to comment on the ideas put forward by all the other members of the group and to help to keep the discussion going. Everyone in the group should take on this role, in addition to their specifically allocated roles, from the previous list.

It is important that each member of a group feels personally responsible for a specific role so that the group can complete the task on time. It is equally important that each member feels collectively responsible for the group output and is willing to play other roles as and when it seems necessary—for example, by commenting on other people's contributions, bringing in additional points, new ideas, and resources.

This posting about roles by Student2 gave the group a starting point to share out their responsibilities. Prior to this, the group was less well organised and focused. In my view, the tutor should organise these roles and tasks. Profiling the learners at an early stage in the course helps the tutor set up the groups. The way the tutor formed the group suggested that he was aware of their gender and background. The following is the tutor's response (msg#285) to comments about the lack of an imposed structure:

> I felt I was imposing enough structure, possibly too much, by dividing folk to groups and by identifying the two context options. I would have felt very uncomfortable about designating individuals to roles, and indeed (I may as well admit) was not quite sure what sort of roles would be needed. There wasn't time in my schedule at the right point to allow for a call for volunteers and for views on a possible cast of actors etc so I made a feature rather than a bug of just getting on a plane and leaving you to it. (message posted June 12, 2000)

The participants' commitment to the task and their shared expectations and behaviour patterns (such as checking frequently for e-mail and conference messages) influence the outcome of any assigned group tasks. Collaboration may suffer if group members leave the group or are unwilling to join the group in the first instance.

The tutor's role in keeping the group focused and engaged is of paramount importance. This is especially the case if it becomes clear that the frequency of visits to the conference system varies within the group. Some group members may check the system frequently, others rarely, and some not at all. The tutor can send e-mail messages to the less active participants and prompt them to contribute. The tutor can also move a student from one group to another as necessary. Student6 (msg#23) voiced concerns about 'what to do with students who don't fit one mould?'. He also argued for individualised learning: 'Online courses will require non-linear construction with pathways that re-connect with the main topic. Teachers need not be told to "modify" for the needy few but rather "individualize" for the class as a whole' (message posted May 20, 2000). I contend that a nonlinear construction is a good fit for individualising the learning, but the institution must consider the design costs and the management of nonlinear tasks as well.

4.2.5. Administration

Administrative support in course H804 was limited to one page of information about the online submission of assignments through the Electronic Tutor Marked Assignment and via e-mail. Students could also download a guide to submitting assignments. Student5 (msg#111) identified the stages of learner support from Freeman (1997)—see table 6.

Student3 (msg#137) highlighted the importance of administrative staff in providing course information, registration, tutor support, information resources, finance, technology, and the student union. She suggested several additional tasks that administrative staff can undertake to support online learners, for example: responding to inquiries, record keeping, facilitating online conferencing, counselling, setting up accounts, administering student loans and payments, despatching material, and issuing passwords. Administrative support was available throughout course H804.

4.2.6. The Learner Profile

In this section, I have looked at learner profiles through a cognitive, metacognitive, affective, and physical framework. Tutors need to see their students as individuals with their own characteristics and attitudes, rather than as a homogonous group. Profiling learners is a complex activity (Evans, 1997):

> The more one knows of the diversity of students' experiences, views and circumstances, the more uncertain one

TABLE 6. Learner support stages.

1. Learner information, guidance, and enrolment
• Precourse information
• In-course information
• Postcourse information
2. Learning resources
• Supply
• Legal issues
• Access
• Administration
• Technology selected
• Effectiveness
3. Learner support
• Lecturers
• Learners
• Support staff
• Learner self-help
4. Lecturer support
5. The assessment system
• Hand-marked assignments
• Computer-marked tests
• Examinations
• Information on the assessment process
6. Monitoring and evaluation
7. Managing the investment

becomes as a teacher or trainer. Previous homogenous conceptions of the student are exploded into a galaxy of individual, unique students. The more one finds out, the more one realizes there remains to find out. It is rather like settling down to sleep under the stars in the Australian desert on a moonless night. As one's eyes become more accustomed to the dark, the stars between the stars become clear. If it wasn't for falling asleep, it appears more stars would be revealed forever. (p. 124)

The establishment of a learner-profile area in an online system is essential to quality teaching and learning. It enables the course leaders to make informed decisions about strategies and approaches to teaching and learning. Tutors and course designers can maximise their contribution and students can begin to know one another's potential.

There were 13 mature adults in this group of students, a mix of male and female students; most were married and had children. No information was provided about any physical disability that might hamper a student in his/her learning. Most of the students were employed in fields related to open and distance education; they wanted to reestablish links with their previous studies and take up again from where they had left off before. Some of them had paid the course fees personally, while others had their fees paid in full or in part by their employer.

The students expected the course to provide them with knowledge for important aspects of their everyday life; some wanted to gain credits towards a university degree without attending classes. We may assume that they had the same fears and worries about studying on a tight schedule in this course, as they had experienced earlier in life. As most of the group had attended courses H801 and H802, they were used to studying at a higher level; they had experience of online and distance learning and of using CME in this context. The students knew the curriculum content and many already had experience of the subject of this module.

The success of the learner-profile area helped to secure a high student retention rate. Most of the H804 group were 'known to one another' from the previous courses, which helped to create effective links and promote good partnership working among them. There was an established relationship between individual thinking and cognition, and between the group interactions, which created joint cognition. The students talked about their experiences of studying courses H801and H802 in eight messages. Sharing these experiences increased the group's social cohesion and motivation. Student2 reflected on her experience of H804:

> What was memorable was the fact that we hadn't looked at the theory but launched into the practice of collaborating. The learning activities resulting in the sharing of knowledge, experiences and skills was very exciting and encouraging within the group. (message posted May 19, 2000)

Because the students were 'known to one another', this enhanced peer-to-peer support:

> I think it is true what John says (msg#88), that we all struggle to keep up with all the work and tasks in these H80* courses. To me, it really helps a lot to know that you and others among my peer students have much the same feelings of shortcoming and pressure as I have. Maybe this emotional aspect is the core part of peer support? (message posted May 24, 2000)

The group 'known to one another' also encouraged one another to ask for pastoral help (msg#15):

> The next instance of tutor support came last year right at the start of H802 when [tutor X] was my tutor. Early in 98, I had started a charity, which was very demanding in the early days when my co-founder and I were on our own. By the time H802 had started, I was under a heavy workload from the charity and my day job. I decided something had to go and it was going to be the OU. I sent [tutor x] an Email to this effect but the reply was to have a profound effect on my thinking. [Tutor x] said, 'That's it then! Just drop out' or words to that effect. He then went

> on to tell me how H802 was right up my street since it dealt with the technology aspects of DL and I would enjoy it. He was so right and I can say that tutor X changed my mind. What amazed me was his understanding of me, we had not been working together that long. (It was March 99) yet he told me how my strengths would help me and others on the course. He pointed out how the course focused on my areas of interest. (message posted May 18, 2000)

The core activity of the CME involves individual members 'who are known to one another' composing text at a networked computer. Course members can read and respond to the topic whenever they choose and wherever they are. An archived network holds the contributions. The effect is the creation of an unfolding written conversation, which offers pedagogical benefits from the discussion. Sustaining a discussion in written words only can be an unusual experience because the normal gestures and facial cues are lacking from the conversation and this may hinder understanding. Most systems offer the facility to attach or index images, sound, and further information, but the capacity of network servers, bandwidth restrictions, or technical skills may constrain the activity.

Being 'known to one another' helped the group to work 'closely', which is a common feature of collaborative learning. The participants helped one another in giving explanations rather than just answers, shared ideas, and considered resources. The closeness of the group enhanced their ability to organise their work on an activity—for example, agreeing on roles and the sequence of actions to accomplish the task. Although the tutor set the roles in the group tasks for H804, the group still had to negotiate these roles and work collaboratively.

'I suggest you use different roles to ensure that each person in the tutor group has a specific contribution to make to the debate, as well as a responsibility to comment on what each person in the group says. Your tutor will suggest how you distribute these roles among members of the group:

- One person as Chair—makes sure the activity actually happens, manages the process
- One person as Proposer of the motion—starts the argument in favour of the motion
- One person as Opposer of the motion—starts the argument against the motion
- One person as Rapporteur—"weaves" the debate and summarises
- Several people as Researcher—brings new evidence/ideas from sources
- All to act as Commenters, in addition to their specific role'. (message posted May 30, 2000)

Although the group collaborated in activities, various external factors influenced the level and type of contributions, for example: insufficient time to participate ('away the coming weekend'; 'I am on holiday') or technical problems ('computer broke down'), which meant that others had to do extra work to complete the activity. Group members were aware of these issues and used e-mail and the conference area to overcome these problems. The H804 course took a semistructured approach to sharing learners' profiles; students responded to an initial thread posted by the tutor:

> [P]lease make a start on Activity 1 ('Who are we?'), and enter something about yourself in the discussion thread below it. The sooner we learn something about each other—or remind ourselves about each other—the easier

> it will be to get the group online activities going. I've
> started off the thread with a few words about myself.
> (message posted May 11, 2000)

The semistructured approach helped the course team to gather
specific information about how and why a particular learner or a
group of learners tackled an activity. For example, it allowed the
tutor to form groups of a similar academic background to tackle a
specific project. Students were able learn more about one another,
find out about shared interests, and relate to one another. Subsequently, they worked more collaboratively in tackling the course.
One problem with this approach is that learners post similar messages in every course they take. Students on course H804 posted
around 90 messages of greeting and stories about themselves.
Another problem with this approach is that learners needed to
search the archive of what fellow students said about themselves
in order to stay engaged with one another, and this could be a
tedious task.

Learner Motivation
Learners' motivation is liable to change to some extent, as other
things happen in the students' lives; motivation is not anchored
permanently in one position. One student listed two reasons for
taking the course:

> This is my fifth OU course, and I think I have had two-
> fold motivation in relation to all of them—I have only
> ever done a course if it has fulfilled both of the following
> criteria:
>
> • the content of the course has been personally inter-
>   esting to me
> • the course has been fairly directly relevant to my job or
>   career development. (message posted May 11, 2000)

Peer support also motivated the participants. Martin (msg#326) commented on the importance of emotional support:

> Thanks, Student4, for these thoughts; and for such a great weaving job. I think you're spot on with your comments about fear and guilt and the emotional support of co-students. Selfish thoughts of survival, I'm afraid, were what caused me to decide not to participate in Act.2. And while the guilt continues, I'm trying not to beat myself up about it too much, as the strategy seems to have been rewarding. Reflective non-participation gave me the space (finally!) to find a focus for the Big Project. And I've decided to look at just that—peer support and feelings of community. (message posted May 20, 2000)

Tutor support is vital in motivating and encouraging learners. Student7 (msg#15) said the following:

> The first instance was during H801 and my tutor was Tutor X******. I found H801 very difficult since it contained a lot of educational theory, which in mind did not map to the real world of business training. I did not realize that this showed up in my posting, but it must have, as one day I got a call from X*****. He noted that I might be finding some of the material difficult and went on to say that I should not worry as many students doing H801 had the same experience. It was not a long call, but it helped as I felt that there was a person I could relate to at the other end of the bulletin board. This simple act of calling a me had the right effect; I stopped worrying and got on with the work. (message posted May 18, 2000)

Student11 (msg#16) saw support as just-in-time medicine: 'Support is not some permanent warm blanket of attention and guidance but well-dosed, sparingly applied just-in-time stimuli that help you on, ever so lightly help-pushing a child on a swing' (message posted May 18, 2000).

CMC provides a rich set of pedagogical tools that tutors can use to motivate online learners. The teaching framework for course H804 was learner centred, resource based, and constructivist; it gave the learner personal control and an awareness of the learning process. Tutors used a wide range of pedagogical techniques:

- a small group approach;
- two-way communication between tutor and learner;
- role plays;
- positive comments and high-quality tutor feedback;
- asynchronous critical reflection;
- self-pacing and self-direction;
- cultural exchange;
- peer-to-peer interaction;
- informal socialisation, the online Café;
- inviting expert speakers; and
- access to online library resources.

The course team responded well to the learners' needs; they were able to steer the learners towards their goal by motivating them to use their innate capabilities and by providing high-level support services.

4.2.7. Technical

Implementing a computer-mediated environment requires careful initial planning and the provision of sustainable technical support throughout the life of the system. Even the best computers are susceptible to crashes and malfunctions. The problem with current technology is that it is insufficiently transparent for learners or tutors. Students are concentrating too much on learning to use the technology and not enough on the course.

The technical-support requirements for an online distance-learning course will depend on what is necessary to sustain a high-quality, networked system. It is possible to develop and deliver online multimedia and customised courses single-handedly, but they will lack the quality derived from a team approach with various types of expertise, for example, the subject expert, the instructional designer, and the multimedia developer.

The technical team for course H804 worked together to support the course and resolve any technical issues that hindered the learning process. All participants, tutors, students, and administrators used e-mail and the conference area for technical problems. A technician allocated to the virtual learning environment dealt with any technical programming issues and problems; for example, the technician provided a voting form for use in the virtual environment when the group asked for this. There was no FAQ ('frequently asked questions') area where technicians could post solutions to recurrent problems; however, this approach might not have been enough support for those who required interactive feedback. Another way of providing active support might have been to provide a help-desk telephone service.

4.3. THE CONVERSATION ZONE

4.3.1. Overview

The teaching strategy in course H804 was based on teacher-student, student-student, and student-content interaction. The model expects that the tutor will supplement the learner's action with constructive feedback and provide students with opportunities for reflection. Laurillard's conversational model (Laurillard, 1993) offers a useful evaluation methodology for computer-mediated systems. The key characteristics that relate to the online environment are the discursive, the adaptive, the interactive, and the reflective modes.

4.3.2. Discursive Tools

Laurillard's conversational framework (Laurillard, 1993) supports constructivist approaches to teaching and learning. Because several characteristics of this conversational model apply to learner support in a computer-mediated communication environment, it provides the best fit for a pedagogical-evaluation framework for learner support in the H804 virtual learning environment.

The basis of course H804 is constructivist teaching and learning methods: the tutor acts as a more capable peer, to assist the learners as they actively negotiate understanding and make meaning of the curriculum content. Discursive interaction makes teachers' and students' ideas accessible to one another; they agree upon the learning topic and task goals together, and the teacher provides an environment in which the student can give and receive feedback appropriate to the topic goals.

Discursive interaction is comparable to a play; the learning environment is proxy to the theatre; the participants are proxy to the actors, where each plays a certain role negotiated among the participants; the tools that participants use—text, graphics, and audio—are synonymous with the actors' play script and props. Each thread within the discursive learning environment is comparable to the dialogue between the characters in a play and contributes towards unfolding the full story represented by the topic under discussion.

One can also compare discursive interaction to an orchestra: the conductor (synonymous with the course team) strives to integrate the group's performance to produce the music.

Between performances, the orchestra members (like students) are free to go their own way until their next practice or performance. The instruments in an orchestra are synonymous with the communication tools in a CME (chat, conference, e-mail, etc.). The orchestra members' access to facilities, administration, and technical support is synonymous with the access and administrative and technical support provided to learners in a CME. Although it is important to have good instruments and musicians, that alone does not guarantee a good performance. Similarly, good technology alone cannot guarantee effective learning.

Table 7 illustrates this process for three of the learners' activities in block H804, and shows how the messages and conversation threads develop.

Table 8 illustrates the process of creating the story among the participants:

Most CMC systems contain tools for conducting conversations; these rely largely on e-mail and asynchronous discussion groups. While the functions within the system itself are important, it is how participants can use these functions to support the conversation that really matters. In course H804, the functionality did not permit direct conversational access between the conference area and the course area; students had to log in and out between these functions in order to continue the conversation.

TABLE 7. Learners' activities.

Activity	No. of messages	No. of threads	Max. Thread Depth
Activity one	59 messages	59 threads	13
Activity two	232 messages	232 threads	15
Activity three	31 messages	31 threads	09

TABLE 8. Story activities.

Scene Name	Learner Support		
Characters	Activity One Contribution	Activity Two Contribution	Activity Three Contribution
Tutor	1 message	11 messages	2 messages
Student1	2 messages	11 messages	None
Student2	6 messages	24 messages	5 messages
Student3	6 messages	25 messages	7 messages
Student4	12 messages	12 messages	9 messages
Student5	1 message	13 messages	None
Student6	1 message	None	None
Student7	6 messages	41 messages	None
Student8	5 messages	8 messages	2 messages
Student9	9 messages	31 messages	2 messages
Student10	2 messages	1 message	None
Student11	3 messages	29 messages	None
Student12	2 messages	20 messages	1 message

Teacher Tools

Discursive interaction begins with the teacher presenting his/her ideas, using online tools. Hansen and Frick (1997) demonstrated diagrammatically a set of tools that developers can use.

These tools include the following:

- sound-file converter,
- video-file converter,
- Web-server account,
- file-transfer program,
- Web browser,
- CGI scripts,
- e-mail system,
- communications,
- HTML text editor,
- graphics editor,

FIGURE 1. Course map.

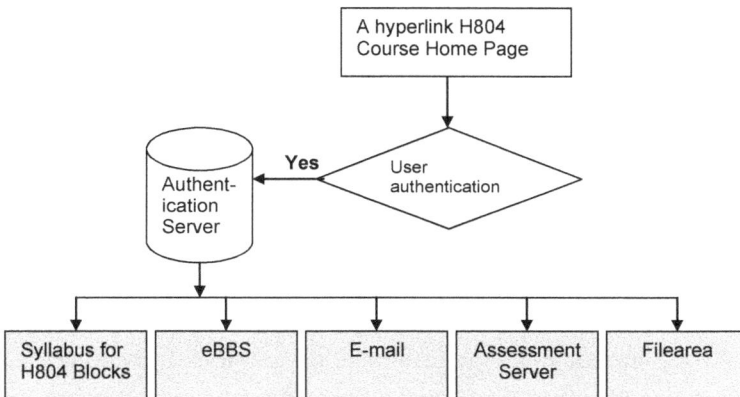

- online spell checker, and
- graphics converter.

However, the course tutor need not be an expert user of all of these tools.

In course H804, the tutors posted, edited, and modified messages posted to the conference area; commented on and graded assignments; responded to students' e-mail; and uploaded and downloaded files to the filearea. As a minimum, the tutors needed to be comfortable using Microsoft Word, e-mail, file-area, and the conferencing system for presenting their ideas. The tutor presented her ideas in a Web page at the start of the block, with hints about tackling the task (msg#0):

> As with earlier Blocks, here is a thread for the general discussion forum/notice board, for each of the Activities, and for the two TMA's due during this Block. I hope these are useful.

> Remember that I am away from 13th to 30th May, but that I hope to be able to get at my email, and reach the H804 pages pretty much as I can now, but perhaps not so often. So, bear with me?

> The main online task in this Block (Activity 2) is a collaborative group one and I would urge you to participate in it as much as you can. As previously, the idea is to support each other as well as developing individual ideas toward TMA04—and beyond. The focus of the Block being 'learner support'. (message posted May 11, 2000)

Course H804 used two of Mason's three models (Mason, 1998a): the wrap-around model with embedded activities and online discussions, and the integrated model, which is characterised by collaborative activities, discussions, and joint assignments.

When the student or the group seeks help or clarification from the tutor, or when the tutor feels that the student has reached a point where s/he needs support, there are several possible options.

- The tutor's first option is to provide a discursive environment where students can act on, generate, and receive feedback on the topic.
- A second option is for the tutor to support students in a process in which they link the feedback to the topic goal at every level of description within the topic threads.
- A third option is for the tutor to provide basic feedback on the actions relating to the topic or task.
- As a fourth option, the tutor can take responsibility for guiding the continuous dialogue.

The instructional framework in course H804 used a 'scaffolding' knowledge construction, in which the course team state their initial position on a topic, gather evidence from Internet resources, provide reflection on the evidence, and invite the group to clarify alternative positions and arguments through an electronic discussion. This example from Block 3 illustrates the point:

> Its a well tuned opinion in my own institution that course teams do far more learning than those who subsequently study the courses they create. I hope, like me, you will choose not to go along with this particular myth, and will sit firmly on the fence with those who say: I've known examples where it felt like it might be true, and some where it didn't, and anyway, how on earth would you really be able to tell? (message posted May 22, 2000)

The H804 online environment had several limitations:

- The design of the online environment employed a modular approach, which comprised the assessment service module, the filearea module, and the eBBs module. Access to each module required a different authentication.
- Although tutors were able to use video and audio clips in the file area, the eBBS did not support the embedding of graphics, charts, and pictures; the tutor had to design a Web page on the OU server, and then provide a link from this to the eBBS.
- The online environment lacked a suite of questions tools for surveys, voting, and questionnaires. When these features were needed, the technician team needed to become involved.

Student Tools

In the H804 online environment, students could view course material, receive instructions and assignments, ask questions via e-mail and the conference area, integrate reading and teaching material, submit assignments and activities to the filearea, and participate in Web-based discussions.

Students needed appropriate tools to present their ideas in this process of knowledge construction. The conference area was the course hub where these tools were available. For example, the facility to post messages and reply to them was very important for the students' collaborative tasks. The OU database server automatically generated a number for each message; the user could reference another message or messages in the conference area by typing the message number preceded by hash sign, which automatically converted it into a hyperlink to the designated message. This feature was not available in over 25 other conferencing groupwares that I examined.

Most course H804 groups were confident in using computers and the tools in the online environment. However, some members did have difficulties with computing jargon. Student1 in msg#50 speaks about his experience, drawing on the work of an open- and distance-education practitioner.

> I remember when I first started learning about using computers that everything was a bit of a mystery. I didn't understand the use of metaphor—I don't think that the so-called 'desktop' looks anything like any work area that I've ever used. Even the simplest of terms—folder, file, C drive/hard drive, clipboard, etc—were by no means transparent. It is not that these things are necessarily difficult but the sheer size of the environment means that some degree of cognitive overload seems inevitable to the brand new user of these things. When this is multiplied through the various programs one has to use—word processors, HTML editors, graphics programs, CMC software and so on it can really be daunting.
>
> To illustrate the point. Last year my company went through a process of standardising its delivery platform.

On the back of this they established a technical help desk run along call centre lines. They underestimated the demand by around 300%. (message posted May 25, 2000)

This experience supports my contention that students should have an induction course on using computer tools prior to commencing their course of study. Learners cannot present their ideas to their tutors and peers until they have mastered the tools; learning how to use unfamiliar tools simultaneously with managing their course workload can disadvantage students who are unfamiliar with the technology.

Discursive tools should facilitate the creation of interactive storyboard frames through which participants can follow a discussion from start to finish. The eBBS had some nice features, which worked well:

- The 'All in one page' feature allowed participants to display all messages in one full Web page, and to save or print all or some of the pages for offline reflection. This feature made it very easy to find specific information within a document, using the 'find' facility in the Web browser.
- The eBBS 'Navigator' feature allowed participants to display an outline of the discussion area and provided directives to the eBBS messages in a compressed form.
- The 'Info' feature provided information about participants and a history of who had read the messages.
- The 'Jump' feature provided a hyperlink to other messages in the conference area, using a unique number.
- The 'New in forum' feature provided a link to all new messages posted to the forum.
- The 'Message heading' feature displayed message headers on the same topic within a node, at the top of the

posted message, and provided a hyperlink to other messages within the topic.

These features helped students to formulate and present their ideas.

Task and Goal Setting

One of the most significant tasks the design team needs to undertake is to set up flexible tasks that allow the student and the tutor to agree on a learning goal. For example, the introduction to Activity 1 gives the student a choice of goals to agree upon with the tutor:

> The rationale for this activity is that it will set you thinking back over your own experience of learner support and so raise questions which you will have in mind, when you work through the various resources and texts.
>
> Think back over your own experience of learner support—whether from the perspective of learner or supporter, and choose one of these experiences, which seems to you to sum up something important about learner support. Post a message to your group which includes two sections, each perhaps a paragraph long:
>
> i. your chosen example of learner support in action
> ii. what it tells you about whether and why learner support is important: does this support or contradict any of your reading of course materials on the topic? (message posted May 11, 2000)

4.3.3. Interactive Tools

Creating an online environment where students can communicate and build knowledge requires creation of interactive interfaces.

Identity

Typically, access to course H804 online required an authenti-cated username and password. The system added the partic-ipant's username automatically to the message header so that others could identify the author of the contribution to the discus-sion; students could not choose alternative names if they wished to do so. In my view, this is a limitation of the system, particu-larly if a student feel that his or her point of view is a minority opinion and could affect subsequent contributions. There is also a fear of 'stealth asymmetry' whereby the participant's name might cause others to limit their interaction with his/her. A study by the University of Chicago the found that '[c]andidates named Emily O'Brien or Neil McCarthy were much more likely to get calls back from potential employers than applicants named Tamika Williams and Jamal Jackson, even though they had the same credentials'[1].

Language differences may cause other forms of 'stealth asymmetry' in a CME. A group of students using their mother tongue might feel superior to other members of the course who are not native speakers; the native speakers could form their own subgroup, and this could deter other students from voic-ing their opinion. A group who are known to one another—for example, from one company or institution—may also form a subgroup and therefore discourage others from full participa-tion. The institution is important here, and the tutor's skill and awareness plays a major role in creating and maintaining a level of symmetry among the group throughout the period of its collaboration. The situation described above could manifest itself with a CME and go unnoticed. It is important to raise awareness of these issues and to carry out more research in this area.

Interactivity

Interactivity comprises action and response. Interactive tools are essential within the online virtual learning environment for conversations among participants; they can use text, audio, and video. The eBBS conferencing software had several features that were helpful in facilitating 'interactivity'—the navigation, history, who's online, hyperlinks, and 'all in one page'.

Interaction between students and the instructor follows a non-linear procedure whereby the instructor posts a message to the conference area to initiate a discussion and invites the students to contribute—for example, giving students directions on how to prepare for the block, and directives about time, contributions, and group formation. The tutor evaluates the students' input and can respond directly to the message initiators or wait until he/she feels that the discussion is drifting from the goal and needs redirection.

The interactive tools available for course H804 were limited to text, filearea, zip files, Microsoft Word documents, e-mail, and textual and graphical hyperlinks. The tutors need to be skilled in using the software in order to create the tasks—for example, they would need the ability to use an authoring tool in order to create Web content. The design team and tutors on course H804 had to ask the programmers for help in creating voting forms, as the virtual online environment did not have this feature.

There were wide differences in how the participants used these tools. Student3's msg#28 recounts one student's experience of trying to access the course area.

> One of my group, a retired teacher, is not yet online for the May presentation. She has phoned ACS so often they say, 'Oh yes, A. Most of us here have spoken to her'. She has phoned me maybe just as often and I have talked her through installation of her disks and accessing the

course Website and First Class many, many times. She
has returned her first OU computer 'because it didn't
work'. She has replacement CD-ROMs. At times she
is close to tears and at pains to tell me that she is well
respected by her former students. 'But what am I doing
wrong, here, Student3?' is her familiar cry. 'It doesn't
work'. (message posted May 19, 2000)

This experience with the technology is very common and suggests that some students do not find it easy to use computer
software. For example, many of my students were new to computers; when they were shown how to start Windows XP and
how supply a username and a password, they were baffled by
the black dotted circles that appear in the password box.

Students on course H804 course accessed the course home page
through a secure Web page, having received their log-in details
by post. After successful log-in to the Web site, learners meet
a welcoming Web page; this comprises seven interactive areas:

- a presentational area, which displays block rationale,
  what is required from students, and a timetable for activities, readings, and assignments;
- a navigational area that represents the dynamic course
  contents in response to clicking a button;
- a group area that represents a dynamic link to the conference area;
- activities link, which represents a dynamic link to current
  block activities;
- a resource link that represent a link to a resource library
  area;
- a link to plenary conference area, which includes a Café
  conference area; and
- a link to the Tutor Marked Assignment area.

The Web page has a date and time stamp, which helps learners to identify any changes and additions. The page also provides a study calendar; course welcome and activities guide; study and assignment guides and reference to external readings; and access to bibliographical databases.

4.3.4. Adaptive Tools

The exchange of ideas between the tutor and the students may require a timed adaptive release to ensure that students remain focused and motivated. This is comparable to a computer game with several levels—when a user achieves level 1, the next level is activated, and so on.

Elements of the course content may not apply to all participants; adaptive release allows the tutor to activate or deactivate the display of material as necessary. It allows the tutor to customise learning paths through the course content and activities, based on criteria such as date and time, specific users, group membership, grades or attempts on a particular test or assignment, or the Review Status of another item in the course.

The four blocks in course H804 were not available to the students simultaneously. The content of the next block was only made available when students were nearing completion of the current block, because the H804 online environment did not have the facility for adaptive release.

Information technology has increased the independence, participation, and productivity of people with diverse abilities; adaptive technology makes it possible for anyone to access computers and the Internet. However, gaining access is not enough. What determines whether the Internet can create a level playing field in accessing information is how well information publishers design their Web site so that they are accessible to a wide audience, including people who are using adaptive technology.

The H804 design team were careful to ensure that the online course was accessible from different hardware systems such as Apple Mac and IBM PCs. The team knew how slowly the Internet loads Web pages that contain graphics, buttons, frames, and animations, and therefore they used a simple, standard page layout throughout. For example, for faster access, they used a text-based menu rather than graphics and image maps, and a Web page template instead of frames for the navigation window. Student1, in msg#50, underlines the importance of this when he states that

> [m]y department provides a technical help desk facility for learners both within the company and clients outside using products we produce. The one thing that it has really taught me is that no interface is transparent to the novice, or even intermediate, user. (A new program we released was very successful: everything was on the screen that the learner had to use—except the print function, which was in a Windows style pull down menu. I won't tell you the number of calls we received.) It has also emphasised how inadequate people feel when confronted with what they think is an inherently simple problem. 'I'm sure that I'm being really stupid but...' is how they often commence.
>
> The upside of this is that the learning curve appears to be rapid once they get going. I have been agitating to get an 'Intro to computers' included on the company induction program but without much success. (And much of this is planned to be put into a DL form anyway.) Perhaps for new more techno literate generation coming through this will be less of a problem.
>
> Thorpe notes the importance of introductory face to face contact and Lewis in Lockwood suggests that these kinds of issues need to be addressed before the course begins. I think that the scale of this problem is often under addressed and inadequately dealt with: even the materials

designed to help the learner into the new world often implicitly require a level of knowledge that may not be present. If you can't make it work nothing else is going to get started. (message posted May 21, 2000)

Course H804 had a special online library, which meant that learners spent less time searching for specific resources. The library provided research papers, journals, and reports, which students could pull out, modify, and replace at any time. Students mentioned the importance of the library support in msg#118, msg#136, msg#137, msg#151, msg#184, msg#194, msg#213, msg#232, msg#255, and msg#262. msg#236 posted by Student1 highlights this point:

> There is quite in a bit in Nazira's library area. I remember reading a concise eval. of conferencing in the OU by Robin Mason. I couldn't find that one but this link is to a paper that seems to cover the same ground. I guess it would be good to have a list of bullet points on ground rules, but maybe this would go against collaborative constructivist theory. (message posted May 19, 2000)

The design team for H804 recognised the diversity of their learners and responded well to their needs by creating a simple interface, supported by the technicians, tutors, and administrators.

4.3.5. Reflective Tools

We can divide the CMC tools (e.g., e-mail, chat, conference, file server, etc.) that foster interaction among the participants in order to provide peer and group interaction into two categories: synchronous and asynchronous tools. Nicholas (1997) stressed the importance of developing suitable formative evaluation techniques, and identifies key differences in access to assistance between conventional and Web-based instruction. Course H804 did not offer participants facilities for chat, video-conferencing, or tele-conferencing I believe that these particular interactive technologies have little impact on learning outcomes. Textual interaction was the main unit of communication in course H804, and reflection was its process. The chat feature could have been a distraction from the course focus and could have been difficult to manage, especially with students working in different time zones. Video conferencing is still in its infancy, and users could spend too much time setting up the technology, to say nothing of the need to understand the protocol of visual communication.

The eBBS and e-mail were the main interactive tools on course H804. However, the course environment did not integrate e-mail within the online delivery system; students were free to use whatever e-mail system they preferred, and this had two implications for the learner and administrator. While it meant less policing, administration, and moderation for the administrator, there could be difficulties if learners failed to notify the administrator and tutors of any change to their e-mail addresses, in which case maintaining e-mail contact with learners becomes impossible. The lack of a generic e-mail facility also made it difficult for learners to access the course from different machines. I am in favour of an integrated e-mail system within a learning environment because of the following points:

- Changes in e-mail addresses are reduced and the exchange of information is likely to be more manageable.
- E-mail messages are saved on the central server instead of being saved on different Internet service providers' e-mail servers. Having e-mail messages in one server might be of good value for researchers and developers.

- One e-mail system gives a sense of belonging to the academic discipline, shapes message contents, and reduces padding. However, it might deter students from posting messages, knowing that their identity details will be shared with people they do not know.
- Learners will be able to refer to one central location for technical help and advice.
- Tutor and students will have a standard e-mail address domain name, for example, a@open.uk or b@open.uk. This approach facilitates the classification of learners with a course, group, and location.

4.4. THE OUTCOMES ZONE

The Outcomes Zone concerns peer and group activities and assignments tools that were available to the participants in course H804. If we regard this evaluative framework as a system consisting of input, process, and output, then we can refer to the Antecedent Zone as the system input, the Conversational Zone as the process, and the Outcomes Zone as its output.

4.4.1. Assignments

The course H804 tutors correct and mark the students' assignments, and participate in online feedback support and discussion on the assignments. The tutor set up two threads for issues on the TMAs (Tutor Marked Assignment). This msg#0, posted by the tutor, provides an area for discussion and feedback on the assignments: 'As with earlier Blocks, here is a thread for the general discussion forum/notice board, for each of the Activities, and for the two TMA's due during this Block. I hope these are useful' (message posted May 3, 2000).

The msg#6, posted by the tutor, delineates the choice of topics that students can select for their assignment:

- The design of assessment procedures for an ODL course on microbes and gene technology.
- A review of potential learning activities and support framework for an ODL course on knowledge working in a health-care context.
- A comparison of learning-support needs in face-to-face or online delivery of a course on computer programming.
- A literature review on the role and implications of gender in online learning.
- An investigation of ODL provision for Aboriginal K–12 students in Canada.
- Design procedures for ODL staff development programmes in Higher Education.
- Critical review of inclusion issues for ODL in Further Education.
- The development and presentation of an action plan for online ODL provision in an HE institution.
- Peer support and learning community development within text-based conferencing environments.
- The establishment of a business case for implementing case-based online training for sales representatives.
- The study and evaluation of the design and development process of a staff development course on Web-based teaching and learning.
- Design, stage one development, and implementation of a learning portal for Independent Financial Advisors.
- Needs analysis study for revision of staff development programme in ODL at an HE institution.

- Investigation and report on a framework for future ODL provision in an HE institution.

There was little discussion among the participants about these examinable components; only four messages were posted under the TMA thread. This suggests that students were more concerned with tackling the assignment than with discussing it.

The eBBS also facilitated the posing and answering of questions and providing students with general feedback about assignments that had already been graded and commented on individually. However, this facility was not well used, which suggests that students felt uncomfortable discussing their work in an area that others could view. It suggests the need for a separate, one-one conference area where tutor and student can have a private conference.

The TMA electronic submission system allowed submission at any hour—the tutor marked the TMA and resubmitted it electronically with feedback to the TMA server, where students could download information; there were fewer errors in recording scores, and confirmation of receipts was partially satisfactory. Students tended to submit their assignments near the cut-off date, which created a bottleneck on the server and resulted in failed submissions. The assessment server could not handle files greater than 1MB without them being zipped. Therefore, students and the tutor needed to know how to use another application to compress their files before submission. The electronic system was taken off-line for 2 hours every morning, which worked against the claim of 24-hour flexibility. As an alternative, students could submit assignments via e-mail, but this meant that they had to learn how to attach files. Some students were unable to attach files larger than 1MB because of the size limitations of their e-mail service providers.

Students had to submit their assignments in one of the recommended formats: Microsoft Word, Microsoft Write, Word Perfect, Rich Text Format, or Plain (ASCII) Text. The assignments submitted in any of these formats were imported into Microsoft Word 6, which the tutor uses to mark the students' work. This approach caused various problems, as software such as Plain (ASCII) did not accept tables and charts. Students also needed the appropriate software to view the feedback on the returned assignments. Although the university provided a free assignment software viewer, this was something else that the students had to download, and it meant extra unnecessary workload.

4.4.2. Activities

Students on course H804 tackled activities either individually or in groups. This example is from the Block 3 welcome Web page:
The structure of activities in Block 3 is seen in table 9.

> In order to lead up to Activity 2, we need to review the literature on learner support and share some of our reactions. (posted May 6, 1999)

Displaying the activities in tabular format presents an optimal sequencing of activities, ensures that no activities are missed,

TABLE 9. Activities structure.

Saturday, May 13th	Activity 1 begins	Friday, May 19th Activity 1 ends
Saturday, May 20th	Activity 2 begins	Friday, June 9th Activity 2 ends
Saturday, June 10th	Activity 3 begins	Friday, June 23rd Activity 3 ends

and that different members of the group can coordinate activities among them. The required outputs specified for the end of each activity and the deadlines kept the team's activities on track.

Participants on the course had two output options available to them: the eBBS conference system and the ftp server. The eBBS conference input system comprised a text-box area, a title, a preview button, a submit button, a combo box for message output in a choice of text or html format, and emoticon dropdown list. Students could key in the message as a comment. The text box accepted basic-text format, but common word-processing features such as spelling and grammar checking, font size, font style, bullets, numbering, and graphics were not available. Students who were familiar with html (hypertext marked language) could use this format to submit their comments. However, students who did not know the html language felt disadvantaged in presenting the information, compared to those who were skilled in the html language. Posted messages were outputted in the conference area in a hieratical style. Each message carried a unique number, which was used successfully in referencing other messages. However, only one message could be sent at a time and no attachments were possible. Students relied on the ftp server to send more than one file.

4.5. SUMMARY

In this chapter, I have analysed the technological tools used in the online environment of course H804, and the process of supporting the student in a computer-mediated environment, through technology applications. I have identified the technical barriers that affect learner support

This chapter demonstrates clearly that the acceptance of new tools and procedures for a computer-mediated environment depends on a mix of technical, organizational, pedagogical, and social factors. Evaluation needs to consider these factors if new technologies are to be incorporated successfully into a learner-support system. We can view the three zones as a set of traffic lights. The Antecedent Zone (red light) provides entry to the Conversational Zone (amber light), where the learning processes take place. Successful outcomes are presented in the Outcomes Zone (green light), which provides the route to further programmes or courses.

Galegher and Kraut (1989) have pointed out that

> the history of experience with telecommunications and computer-based information systems contains many instances of expensive technological failures that are at least partly attributable to designs that do not mesh well with the social and behavioural systems in which they are to be used. (p. 489)

Course H804 had a simple online-learning environment and relied mainly on textual interaction. However, a different context that required rich media would necessitate further examination of the groupware.

ENDNOTE

1. Retrieved April 12, 2007, from http://www.cnn.com/2006/US/12/
12/racism.poll/index.html.

CHAPTER 5

CONCLUSION:
CHALLENGES IN PROVIDING
LEARNER SUPPORT

5.1. CHAPTER OVERVIEW

The theme of this book is learner support, and my contention is that technology alone is insufficient to support learners. Most academic institutions have been swift to buy expensive technology, believing that this is enough to deliver online learning. I suggest that this thinking is ill advised, and is more likely to harm online learning than to benefit it.

The online-learning environment is going through an exciting period of change, particularly in communication technology; and the governance of that technology is still developing. Will we continue to derive benefits from using communication technologies for learner support? I believe so, but only if governments and regulators make a concerted effort to establish standards for online teaching and learning. The Open University's mission has prompted a need to explore innovation, especially in the field of models for e-learning. The online Masters Degree in Open and Distance Education is one outcome from such innovation, and is designed to meet the needs of online learners.

In the previous chapters, I examined insights and reflections from messages posted to the conference area of the eBBs by practitioners in Open and Distance Education. This chapter focuses on those aspects of the computer-mediated environment that present a special challenge to academics in the design and implementation of computer-mediated learner-support systems. I have structured this chapter around the four dimensions of the e-learning framework already discussed in chapter 3—the organisational, social, pedagogical, and technical dimensions, which play an integral role in the operation of a computer-mediated system.

5.2. ORGANISATIONAL

In this section, I consider the institution, staff, technicians, course team, and the designers and developers of instructional material, which constitute the practical context underpinning online learning.

5.2.1. The Institution

The global capability of the Web presents challenges in creating meaningful learning environments, and in keeping abreast of changing technologies. Within a distance-learning environment, the diversity of the online learners and their thinking processes presents a further challenge.

Conclusion 151

The evidence I gathered from my research shows that the Open University has successfully taken national priorities, concerns, and developments into account when developing its strategic objectives for online learning. The course-development team demonstrated an informed and progressive vision for increasing learning opportunities, building students' self-esteem, and equipping the diverse groups of learners to participate in their communities and workplaces. There was demonstrable evidence of the course team's effectiveness and of its supportive and collaborative role in enriching the learners' experiences.

An institution's existing technological infrastructure exerts a considerable influence on media selection. There is evidence of academic institutions buying expensive technologies that they fail to explore and use fully.[1] The need to bridge the staff's knowledge gap on the capabilities of their existing infrastructure can be a major challenge to the institution. Institutions need to be proactive in securing the funding necessary to provide high-quality learner support through information technology. The Open University relies on research and development and on collaboration with its partners to position the institution as a leader in the e-learning arena. As the Web and other interactive technologies continue to grow, this will remain an important criterion of success, in delivering online learning.

5.2.2. The Staff

An important aspect of course H804 was the course team's skills in using technology to interface with their students. The University staffed the H804 course at an appropriate level. As the size of the group is important to the success of an online course, the University divided the 40 learners among 4 tutors. A larger group would have made it difficult to use and manage

152 COMPUTER-MEDIATED ENVIRONMENT

the conference area because it would have become too difficult to follow and threads and topics.

Each tutor had the support of a technician, an administrator, a librarian, and a chairperson. The collaboration among tutors and their support for one another was visible through their contribution to the conference area. For example, one tutor might have posted a topic for discussion, which was the four groups then shared. There was evidence to suggest that the teaching, technical, and administrative staff had good knowledge of the quality policies, standards, and procedures in their area of responsibility.

The Open University has shown commitment to staff development and has provided opportunities for staff to achieve their potential. For example, tutors work through an induction programme, and there is evidence of continuous professional development activities (CPD) in the Itinerary conference area.

5.2.3. The Course Design

The theory and practice of online education influenced the overall design of course H804. Most theories of learning suggest that the learning needs to be active if it is to be effective. Active learning engages students in a deeper approach to learning. Course H804 focused on engaging the students in the learning process, and therefore the basis for instruction was designed to exploit the interactivity of the online environment, enabling students to participate in active learning and build complex schemata.

The constructivist approach of course H804 reduced the need to upload the whole course for online consumption. The themes relevant to the instructional design of the H804 context were:

- *Connectedness*: creating an environment that keeps learners connected throughout the learning process;

- *Autonomy and independence*: creating an independent learner by giving control;
- *Negotiation*: learning is negotiated through perspectives and consensus;
- *Sharing*: knowledge is shared to maximise learners' potential; and
- *Control*: learners act as producers of knowledge rather than receptors.

The course design provided multiple opportunities for learners to reflect, organise, create, and publish their own thoughts and resources. Therefore, the learner's role changed from observer to producer through the personal representation of knowledge, influenced by his/her experiences.

The eBBS Conference System

Programmers at the Open University developed the eBBS, and its design was an important factor in encouraging students to participate in active learning. The interface had simple functions such as topic listings, an 'all in one page' view of messages, the posting of HTML messages, and a search facility. It was easy to use. This simplicity demonstrates that expensive software is not necessary to support learning effectively.

An important advantage of having an in-house conference system is having control of it. The Open University programmers were able to modify and update the environment as learners' needs changed. For example, learners demanded a voting system that allowed them to participate in an end-of-topic debate. Some learners suggested the addition of other functions that they felt would enhance their participation, such as a spell checker, e-mail notification, the facility to attach files, and formatting toolbars.

Another advantage of the eBBS was that the programmers developed it to meet the needs of the particular educational context. The eBBS system was simple and well suited for the H804 context, and students were able to respond to the learning material in different ways. The Web interface, which formed the entry point to the conference area, followed a simple structure. There were few Web pages pertaining to the whole course.

The evaluation of the learning outcomes was through students' assignments. Tutors uploaded assignments to an assessment server through a secure-access Web service. Students were able to retrieve their marked assignment using the same process; they received an automatic generated number as evidence of the successful submission of an assignment. The assessment server rejected assignments submitted after the cut-off date, but most students tended to submit their assignments a couple of days before this point. This led to an increase in traffic on the assessment server, which proved unable to cope because of limitations on the bandwidth, and consequently, it did not function well. The online environment was out of service on a few occasions, and students complained about the weaknesses in the technology. There was no 'mirror' online environment in place when the online environment was out of service. The technology failure affected students' participation in active learning.

5.3. SOCIAL

Recognising the importance of social interaction within a virtual learning environment, the H804 design team created a suitable social environment for formal and informal interaction. The online tutors established a protocol for communication because text was the main tool available for conversation. A 'netiquette' Web page provided guidance on the 'dos and don'ts'.

The H804 learner environment emphasised the importance of the individual and encouraged group collaboration and rapport. The Café conference area allowed students to meet outside the formal course area. Messages of congratulations, welcome, advice, and encouragement played a vital part in binding the participants together in collaboration and cooperation. The formal conference area provided links to Web sites created by the students, facilities for posting pictures, and provided an environment for sharing personal experiences. The tutors played an important role in keeping the discourse on track despite the absence of the usual visual and verbal cues. For example, the tutor would intervene if she/he saw that the discussion was becoming heated, or when a misunderstanding arose among participants.

5.4. PEDAGOGICAL

Pedagogical issues concern the principles of teaching and learning. The attention to pedagogy is what differentiates the virtual learning environment of course H804 from other virtual learning environments, which academics use simply for publishing material—the posting of courses and lecture notes. Lockwood (1995) identified three pedagogical principles: engagement, intelligibility, and participation. Course H804 implemented these well.

Dialogue as the basis for pedagogy is vital to the negotiation of shared meaning among participants. Laurillard (1993) proposed a constructivist definition of academic knowledge, differentiating this from everyday knowledge:

> Academic knowledge is not like other kinds of everyday knowledge. Teaching is essentially a rhetorical activity, seeking to persuade students to change the way they experience the world...The learning process must be

constituted as a dialogue between teacher and student, operating at the level of descriptions of actions in the world, recognizing the second-order character of academic knowledge. (p. 28)

Course H804 implemented a knowledge-building technique that emphasised collaboration and interaction. Collaboration among participants came through building knowledge domains, scaffolding, sequencing instructions, conversation and exploration, peer collaboration and interaction, and reflection. Information poured in from different members of the group with hyperlinks, listserv quotes, tables, graphics, and files uploaded to the server, which led to information overload.

Careful course design should incorporate themes for interaction and discussion. The H804 course team applied a scaffolding technique, in a framework that students understood well. Each topic started with a welcome message from the tutor encouraging contributions from participants. The tutor's role was to provide direction, keep learners on 'the right path', to advise, encourage, and to provide synthesis and a summary closure at the end of a topic. At some points, the tutor divided the group into subgroups and assigned them different roles. The tutors were able to identify individuals who did not fit well within a group, and moved them to a different group. The tutors responded well to the different messages posted by the students.

5.5. TECHNICAL

The reliability of the technology in carrying messages backwards and forwards is a critical factor in the learning process. If the technology keeps breaking down, it will fall into disfavour with users very swiftly. The technical team for course H804 worked closely with the design team on the online environment.

The technical team was available throughout the course to resolve connectivity problems and software and hardware queries from learners. The technical support for this course included notifying students if the service was down, providing a maintenance schedule, creating workspace areas, creating conference areas, organising Web course resources and hyperlinks, creating upload and download areas, and creating voting forms.

Students may face many technical problems with online access, including difficulties with broadband connection, hardware, software, and viruses. Technicians can resolve many technical support queries by telephone, by e-mail, through live online help, by posting answers to frequently asked questions (FAQs), or in conference discussion areas. There is a need for more research on who provides this type of support, who bears the cost, and the roles played by those involved in providing this support.

5.6. CONCLUSION

Computer-mediated communication technologies have the potential to create dynamic learner-centred virtual communities. Within certain contexts, they can provide excellent teaching and learning that surpasses conventional education. Technology is important in connecting learners, but it does not 'make' learning. Successful exploitation of the technology depends upon the tutors' ability to promote student engagement in the learning process. The four dimensions of e-learning examined earlier are closely interconnected, and a weakness in any one dimension will affect learner support in all the others.

Claims that the success of technology applications depends only on the purchase and installation of equipment, the hiring of network managers and technicians, and the training of teaching staff in virtual learning environments are ill conceived, and they are harming online education rather than enhancing it. Successful implementation requires a paradigm shift from conventional learning to online learning through careful understanding of the organisational, social, pedagogical, and technical dimensions.

CME technology presents a challenging new stage in providing learner support, particularly in understanding and addressing the physical barriers and psychological aspects of the learners' situation. The CME tool should overcome the physical barriers by supporting dialogue effectively, helping the tutor to understand students' character, habits, and preferences, and to observe the participants' interactions in the online environment.

This study adopts a holistic approach, drawing on the illuminative and integrative methodologies espoused by Parlett and Hamilton (1977). This involved collecting data directly from messages posted by the learners themselves, a methodology that aligns closely with supporting the learner in a virtual communication system. In seeking to answer the question 'How can those elements of an ODL system and other interactive technological features be used, to respond to a known learner or group of learners?', and to contextualise this research, I considered the institution, the stakeholders, the technology, and the learner profile.

In seeking to answer the question 'What is needed to provide the best and most meaningful learner support with CME?', I have studied the literature on e-learning and used a variety of sources. I have interviewed learners, instructors, administrators, and other academic support staff from various institutions who have been involved in the design, development, implementation, and delivery of e-learning over the last decade. I have identified various attributes and features of online-learning tools and shown how participants use these tools. I have also provided a new definition of learner support. From the research for this book, I have discovered that learner support in CME demands a paradigm shift from strategic decision makers, administrators, instructor, technical, and other support services, as well as from learners.

My study examined many factors that may influence learner support in computer-mediated environment courses, and showed that pedagogical and technological factors were those mostly closely associated with students' learning. This could give sceptics some cause for optimism, but it is evident that there is a need for further research in understanding the online learner, and how best to provide effective support. There is fragmented research on e-learning design, e-learning approaches, e-learning structures, e-learning methods, e-learning media types, e-learning pedagogy, and particularly learner support. However, most of this research focuses on the conventional context, and on how it compares with the online context. I contend that academics need to see online learning as a separate paradigm in education. Tutors who deliver online courses must improve their pedagogical skills continually, and make personal and professional investment in maintaining high standards in this rapidly changing environment.

ENDNOTE

1. See http://www.scotland.gov.uk/library/documents-w7/sffe-04.html.

THE LEARNER PROFILE IN CMC

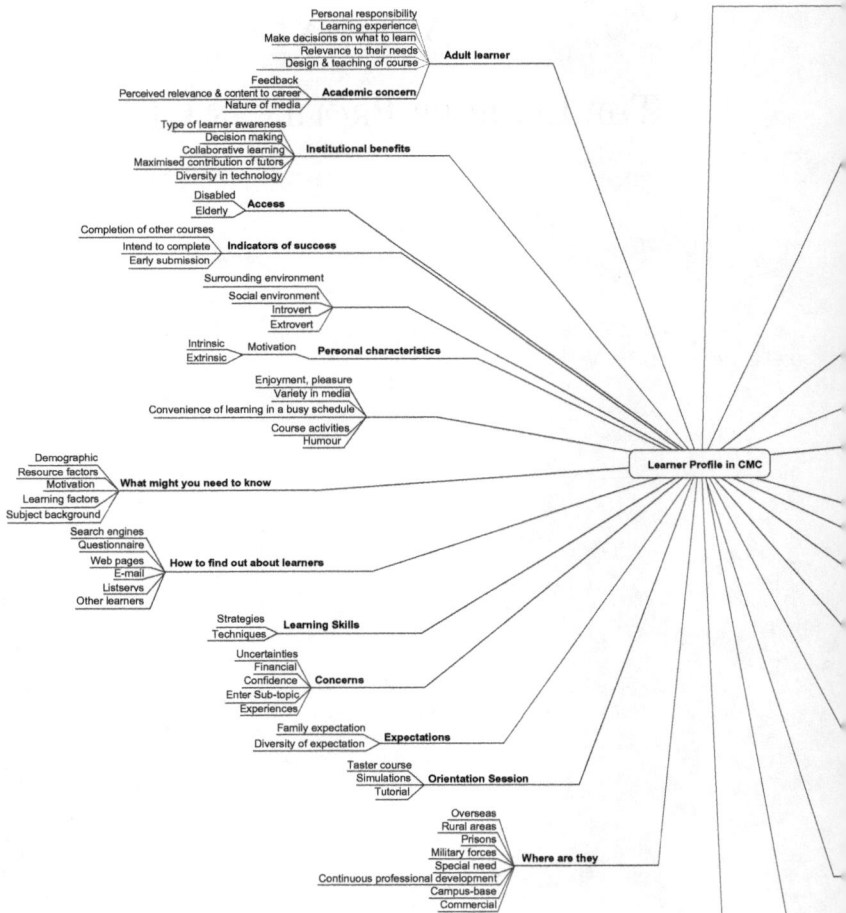

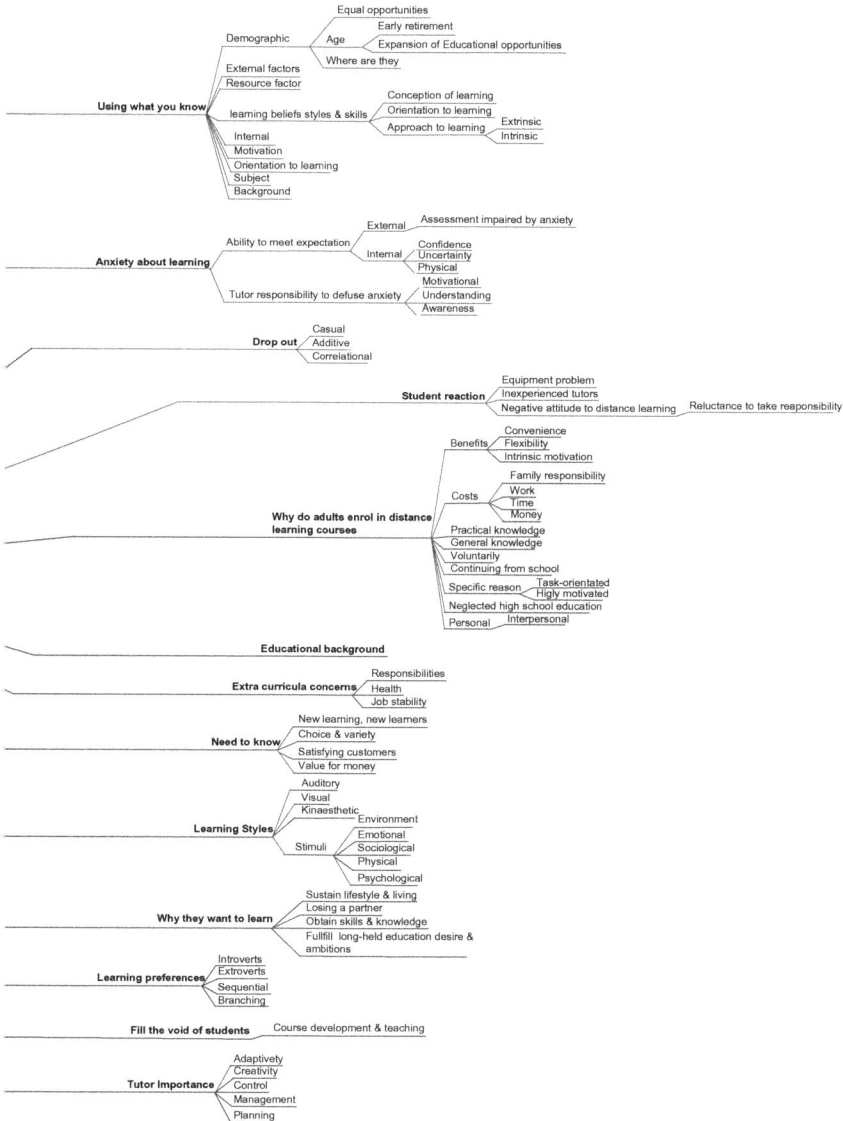

Using what you know

- External factors
  - Demographic
    - Equal opportunities
    - Age
      - Early retirement
      - Expansion of Educational opportunities
    - Where are they
  - Resource factor
- Internal
  - learning beliefs styles & skills
    - Conception of learning
    - Orientation to learning
    - Approach to learning
      - Extrinsic
      - Intrinsic
  - Motivation
  - Orientation to learning
  - Subject
  - Background

Anxiety about learning

- Ability to meet expectation
  - External
    - Assessment impaired by anxiety
  - Internal
    - Confidence
    - Uncertainty
    - Physical
- Tutor responsibility to defuse anxiety
  - Motivational
  - Understanding
  - Awareness

Drop out
- Casual
- Additive
- Correlational

Student reaction
- Equipment problem
- Inexperienced tutors
- Negative attitude to distance learning — Reluctance to take reaponsibility

Why do adults enrol in distance learning courses
- Benefits
  - Convenience
  - Flexibility
  - Intrinsic motivation
- Costs
  - Family responsibility
  - Work
  - Time
  - Money
- Practical knowledge
- General knowledge
- Voluntarily
- Continuing from school
- Specific reason
  - Task-orientated
  - Higly motivated
- Neglected high school education
- Personal
  - Interpersonal

Educational background

Extra curricula concerns
- Responsibilities
- Health
- Job stability

Need to know
- New learning, new learners
- Choice & variety
- Satisfying customers
- Value for money

Learning Styles
- Auditory
- Visual
- Kinaesthetic
- Stimuli
  - Environment
  - Emotional
  - Sociological
  - Physical
  - Psychological

Why they want to learn
- Sustain lifestyle & living
- Losing a partner
- Obtain skills & knowledge
- Fullfill long-held education desire & ambitions

Learning preferences
- Introverts
- Extroverts
- Sequential
- Branching

Fill the void of students — Course development & teaching

Tutor Importance
- Adaptively
- Creativity
- Control
- Management
- Planning

REFERENCES

Aalto, P., & Jalava, M. (1995). Implementing experiences from small-scale courses to large educational systems. In F. Lockwood (Ed.), *Open and distance learning today* (pp. 255–264). London: Routledge.

Adar, L. (1975). *A theoretical framework for the study of motivation in education.* Jerusalem: Hebrew University.

Ahearn, T., Peck, K., & Laycock, M. (1992). The effects of teacher disclosure in computer-mediated discussion. *Journal of Educational Computing Research, 8,* 291–309.

Baath, J. (1980). *Postal two-way communication in correspondance education: An empirical investigation.* Malmo, Sweden: University of Lund, Liber Hermods.

Bates, A. (1997). *Technology, open learning and distance education.* New York: Routledge.

Beard, R., & Senior, I. (1980). *Motivating students.* London: Routledge and Kegan Paul.

Benbunan-Fitch, R., & Hiltz, R. (1999). Impacts of asynchronous learning networks on individual and group problem solving: A field experiment. *Group Decision and Negotiation, 8*(5), 409–426. Retrieved June 24, 2006, from http://www.ainresearch.org.data_files/articled/full_text/benbunan.hrm

Berelson, B. (1953). *Content analysis in communication research.* New York: Free Press.

Berge, Z. (1995). *The role of the online instructor/facilitator.* Retrieved February 23, 2006, from http://cac.psu.edu/~mauri/moderate/teach_online.html

Berge, L., & O'Rourke, J. (1998). The dynamics of distance teaching: Voices from the field. In C. Latchem & F. Lockwood (Eds.), *Staff development in open and flexible learning* (pp. 193–202). London: Routledge.

Bilston, B. (1989). Teaching the older learner. *Adults Learning, 1*(1), 13–15.

Bligh, D. (1972). *What's the use of lectures?* London: Penguin Books.

Bonk, C., & Reynolds, D. (1997). Learner-centered Web instruction for higher-order thinking, teamwork, and apprenticeship. In B. Khan (Ed.), *Web-based instruction* (2nd ed., pp. 167–174). Englewood Cliffs, NJ: Educational Technology Publications.

Bonwell, C., & Eison, J. (1991). *Active learning: Creating excitement in the classroom* (ASHE-ERIC Higher Education Report No. 1). Washington, DC: Jossey Bass.

Brandon, D., & Hollingshead, A. (1999). Collaborative learning and computer-supported groups. *Communication Education, 48*(2), 109–193.

British Educational Research Association (BERA). (2004). *Revised ethical guidelines for education research.* Retrieved June 23, 2005, from http://www.bera.ac.uk/publications/pdfs/ETHICAL

Campbell, D., & Stanley, J. (1966). *Experimental and quasi-experimental designs for research.* Chicago: Rand McNally.

Chambers, E. A. (1993). The role of the theories of discourse in course design for humanities distance education. *Media and Technology for Human Resource Development, 5*(3), 177–196.

Cochran-Smith, M. (1995). Uncertain allies: Understanding the boundaries of race and teaching. *Harvard Educational Review 65*(4).

Colbeck, C., Campbell, S., & Bjorklund, S. (2000). Grouping in the dark: What college students learn from group projects. *Journal of Higher Education, 71*(1), 60–83.

collaboration. (2007). In *Wikipedia: The Free Encyclopedia.* Retrieved March 26, 2007, from http://en.wikipedia.org/wiki/ Collaboration

Collis, B. (1993). Evaluating instructional applications of tele-communication in distance education. *Educational and Training Technology International, 30*(3), 268.

Collis, B. (1997). *Tele-learning in a digital world: The future of distance learning.* London: International Thomson Computer Press.

Creanor, L. (2006). *The learner's voice: A focus on the e-learner experience.* Glasgow, U.K.: Caledonian University, the Open Learning Partnership.

Department for Education and Skills. (2005). *E-strategy— Harnessing technology: Transforming learning and children's services.* Retrieved October 12, 2006, from http://www.dfes. gov.uk/publications/e-strategy/

Dillenbourg, P., & Baker, M. (1996, June 12–14). *Negotiation spaces in human-computer collaborative learning.* Paper presented at the International Conference on Cooperative Systems (COOP 6), Juan-Les-Pins, France.

Donaldson, J. F. (1990). *Managing credit programs in continuing higher education*. Portland, OR: Frank Amato Publications.

Dunn, R., & Dunn, K. (1993). *Teaching secondary learners through their individual learning styles*. Boston: Allyn and Bacon.

Entwistle, N., McCune, V., & Hounsell, J. (2002). Enhancing teaching and learning environments in undergraduate courses. *Universities of Edinburgh, Coventry and Durham: Enhancing Teaching-Learning Environments in Undergraduate Courses (ETL) Project, Occasional Reports, 1.*

Evans, T. (1997). *Understanding learners in open and distance education*. London: Kogan Page.

Feenberg, A. (1989). The written world. In D. Rowntree (Ed.), *The tutor's role in supporting distance learners via computer conferencing* (pp. 12–24). Milton Keynes, U.K.: The Open University.

Ferguson, D. (2001). *Using the 'seven principles for good practice in undergraduate education', WebCT: A practical approach*. Atlanta: Georgia State University, Distance and Distributed Learning.

Fielding, M. (2004). Student voice and personalized learning: A presentation to the Specialist Schools Trust and Secondary Heads Association. In R. Tim, F. Colligan, &, R. Naik (Eds.), *Futurelab handbook* (pp. 3–5). Retrieved February 23, 2007, from http://www.futurelab.org.uk/research/handbooks/04_02.htm

Freeman, R. (1997). *Managing open systems: Managing information, guidance, and enrolment*. London: Kogan Page.

Freeman, R. (1998). *Staff development for project management and quality assurance*. In C. Latchem & F. Lookwood (Eds.), *Staff development in open and flexible learning* (pp. 263–275). London: Routledge.

Galegher, J., & Kraut, R. (1989). *Computer-mediated communication for intellectual teamwork: A field experiment in group writing* (Mimeo). Tucson: University of Arizona.

Gagne, R., Briggs, L., & Wager, W. (1992). *Principles of instructional design.* New York: Harcourt Brace Jovanovich.

Gillani, B., & Relan, A. (1996). Web-based distance learning and teaching: Incorporating interactivity and multimedia into Web-based instruction. In B. Khan (Ed.), *Web-based instruction* (2nd ed., p. 232–240). Englewood Cliffs, NJ: Educational Technology Publications.

Guba, E. (1981). Criteria for assessing the trustworthiness of naturalistic inquiries. *Educational Technology Research and Development, 29*(2), 76.

Guba, E. (1992). Relativism. *Curriculum Inquiry, 22*(1), 22.

Hamel, J., Dufour, S., & Fontin, D. (1993). *Case study methods.* Newbury Park, CA: Sage Publications.

Hammersley, M. (1993). Case study on social research. In *DEH313 principles of social and educational research, block 2, unit 7.* Milton Keynes, U.K.: The Open University.

Hannum, W., & Briggs, L. (1997). *Web-Based Instruction (WBI):* Incorporating interactivity and multimedia into Web-based instruction. In B. Khan (Ed.), *Web-based instruction* (p. 41). Englewood Cliffs, NJ: Educational Technology Publications.

Hansen, L., & Frick, T. (1997). Evaluation guidelines for Web-based course authoring systems. In B. Khan (Ed.), *Web-based instruction* (2nd ed., pp. 299–306). Englewood Cliffs, NJ: Educational Technology Publications.

Harasim, L. (1999). A framework for online learning: The Virtual-U. *Computer, 32*(9), 44–49.

Harasim, L., Calvert, T., & Groeneboer, C. (1997). Virtual-U: A Web-based system to support collaborative learning. In B. Khan (Ed.), *Web-based instruction* (2nd ed., p. 151). Englewood Cliffs, NJ: Educational Technology Publications.

Harasim, L. M., Hiltz, R., Teles, L., & Turoff, M. (1995). *Learning networks: A field guide to teaching and learning online.* Cambridge, MA: MIT Press.

Haughey, M., & Anderson, T. (1998). *Networked learning: The pedagogy of the Internet.* Montreal, Quebec, Canada: McGraw-Hill.

Hawkridge, D. (1995, June). An agenda for evaluation of distance education. In D. Sewart (Ed.), *One world many voices: Quality in open and distance learning. Selected papers from the 17th World Conference of the International Council for Distance Education, Birmingham, UK* (Vol. 2, pp. 348–351). Oslo, Norway: International Council for Distance Education.

HEFCE. (2003). *Consultation on HEFCE e-learning strategy.* Retrieved October 20, 2006, from http://www.hefce.ac.uk/pubs/cirlets/2003/cl21_03/cl21_03.pdf

HEFCE. (2005). *HEFCE strategy for e-learning, 2005.* Retrieved October 29, 2006, from http://www.hefce.ac.uk/pubs/hefce/2005/05_12/05_12.doc

Herring, S. (1993). Gender and democracy in computer-mediated communication. *Electronic Journal of Communication, 3*(2), 10–20.

Hill, J. R. (1997). Distance learning environments via the World Wide Web. In B. Khan (Ed.), *Web-based instruction* (2nd ed., pp. 75–78). Englewood Cliffs, NJ: Educational Technology Publications.

Hiltz, S. (1994). *The virtual classroom: Learning without limits via computer networks*. Norwood, NJ: Ablex Publishing Corporation.

Holmberg, B. (1988). Guided didactic conversation in distance education. In D. Sewart, D. Keegan, & B. Holmberg (Eds.), *Distance education: International perspectives* (pp. 114–122). New York: Routledge.

Honey, P., & Mumford, A. (1986). *The manual of learning styles*. Maidenhead, Berkshire, U.K.: Peter Honey.

Howe, K. R. (2005). The education science question: A symposium. *Educational Theory, 5*(3), 235–321.

Howe, K., & Eisenhardt, M. (1990). Standards for qualitative (and quantitative) research: A prolegomenon. *Educational Researcher, 19*(4).

Jeong, H., & Chi, M. (1999). *Constructing shared knowledge during collaboration and learning*. Poster presented at the AERA Annual Meeting, Montreal, Quebec, Canada.

JISC, (2006). *Learner experiences of e-learning*. The proceedings of theme 2 of the JISC Online Conference: Innovating e-learning 2006. http://www.jisc.ac.uk/media/documents/programmes/elearningpedagogy/ebooktheme2_a4.pdf

Jonassen, D., & Grabowski, B. (1993). *Handbook of individual differences: Learning and instructions*. Hillsdale, NJ: Lawrence Erlbaum Associates.

Juler, P. (1998). Interaction in open and distance education. In *Open University course book H801, block 1, section 1* (p. 132). Milton Keynes, U.K.: The Open University.

Kaplan, B., & Maxwell, J. A. (1994). Qualitative research methods for evaluating computer information systems. In J. G. Anderson,

C. E. Aydin, & S. J. Jay (Eds.), *Evaluating health care information systems: Methods and applications* (p. 132). Thousand Oaks, CA: Sage Publications.

Kaye, T. (1992). *Computer networking for the development of distance education courses [1]* (Paper). Milton Keynes, U.K.: The Open University, Institute of Educational Technology.

Kearsley, G. (1996). *Distance education: A systems view*. Belmont, CA: Wadsworth Publishing Company.

Khan, B. (1997). *Web-based instruction* (2nd ed.). Englewood Cliffs, NJ: Educational Technology Publications.

Khan, B. (2005). *Managing e-learning strategies: Design, delivery, implementation, and evaluation*. Hershey, PA: Information Science Publishing.

Klimoski, R., & Mohammed, S. (1994). Team mental model: Construct or metaphor. *Journal of Management, 20*(2), 403–437.

Koschmann, T. (1996). Paradigm shifts and instructional technology: An introduction. In T. Koschmann (Ed.), *CSCL: Theory and practice of an emerging paradigm* (pp. 1–23). Mahwah, NJ: Lawrence Erlbaum Associates.

Latchem, C., & Lockwood, F. (1998). *Staff development in open and flexible learning: An enabling role*. London: Routledge.

Laurillard, D. (1993). *Rethinking university teaching: A framework for the effective use of educational technology*. London: Routledge.

Laurillard, D. (2002). *Rethinking university teaching: A framework for the effective use of educational technology* (2nd ed.). London: Routledge.

Lave, J., & Wenger, W. (1991). *Situated learning: Legitimate peripheral participation*. Cambridge, U.K.: Cambridge University Press.

Lockwood, F. (1995). *Open and distance learning today*. London: Routledge.

Malikowski, S. (1997). Web-based distance learning and teaching: Interacting in history's largest library: Web-based conferencing tools. In B. Khan (Ed.), *Web-based instruction* (2nd ed., p. 284). Englewood Cliffs, NJ: Educational Technology Publications.

Mandell, A., & Herman, L. (1996). From teachers to mentors: Acknowledging openings in the faculty role. In R. Mills & A. Tait (Eds.), *Supporting the learner in open and distance learning* (pp. 3–16). London: Pitman Publishing.

Manpower Services Commission. (1984). *A new training initiative*. Sheffield, U.K.: Manpower Services Commission.

Marton, F., & Saljo, R. (1984). Approaches to learning. In F. Marton, D. Hounsell, & N. Entwistle (Eds.), *The experience of learning* (p. 46–48). Edinburgh, U.K.: Scottish Academic Press.

Mason, R. (1998a). *Globalising education: Trends and applications: Students and technology-mediated education*. London: Routledge.

Mason, R. (1998b). Models of online courses. *ALN Magazine 2*(2). Retrieved May 20, 2005, from http://www.aln.org/alnweb/magazine/vol2_issue2/Masonfinal.htm

Mayes, T. (2006). *LEX, the learner experience of e-learning* (Methodology report). Retrieved March 12, 2006, from http://www.jisc.ac.uk/media/documents/programmes/elearning_pedagogy/lex_method_final.doc

McMann, G. (1994, April 27–29). The changing role of moderation in computer mediated conferencing. In *Proceedings of the Distance Learning Research Conference*, San Antonio, TX (pp. 159–166). College Station, TX: Department of Educational Human Resource Development, Texas A&M University.

Mills, R., & Tait, A., Eds. (1996). *Supporting the learner in open and distance learning*. London: Pitman Publishing.

Moore, M. G. (1993). Theory of transactional distance. In R. Mills, & A. Tait (Eds.), *Supporting the learner in open and distance learning* (p. 64). London: Pitman Publishing.

Morgan, A. (1993). *Improving Your Students' Learning*. London: Kogan Page.

Nicholas, G. (1997). Formative evaluation of Web-based instruction. In B. Khan (Ed.), *Web-based instruction* (2nd ed., pp. 299–306). Englewood Cliffs, NJ: Educational Technology Publications.

Nipper, S. (1989). Third generation distance learning and computer conferencing. In R. Mason & A. Kaye (Eds.), *Mindweave: Communication, computers, and distance education* (pp. 23–40). London: Pergamon Press.

Parlett, M., & Dearden, G. (1977). *Introduction to illuminative evaluation: Studies in higher education*. Sacramento, CA: Pacific Soundings Press.

Parlett, M., & Hamilton, D. (1977). Evaluation as illumination. In M. Parlett (Ed.), *Introduction to illuminative evaluation: Studies in higher education*. Scotland, U.K.: Pacific Soundings Press.

Paul, R., & Brindley, J. (1996). Supporting the learner in open and distance learning. In R. Mills & A. Tait (Eds.), *Lessons from distance education for the university of the future* (pp. 43–54). London: Pitman Publishing.

Paulsen, M. (1995). *Teaching techniques for computer-mediated communications (CMC)*. Oslo, Norway: NKI.

Perraton, H. (1995). Proposed international research foundation for open learning. *ICDL Update, 5*, 1–2.

Peters, O. (1998). *Learning and teaching in distance education: Distance and proximity*. London: Kogan Page.

Reid, K., Flowers, P., & Larkin, M. (2005). Exploring lived experience. *The Psychologist, 18*(10), 20–23.

Ritchie, D., & Hoffman, B. (1997). Incorporating instructional design principles with the World Wide Web: Revolutionary invention or reaction to necessity? In B. Khan (Ed.), *Web-based instruction* (2nd ed., p. 135–138). Englewood Cliffs, NJ: Educational Technology Publications.

Robinson, B. (1995). Research and pragmatism in learner support. In F. Lockwood (Ed.), *Open and distance learning today* (pp. 221–226). New York: Routledge.

Rogers, C. (1969). *Freedom to learn*. Columbus, OH: Merrill.

Rogoff, B. (1991). Social interaction as apprenticeship in thinking: Guided participation in spatial planning. In L. Resnick, J. Levine, & S. Teasley (Eds.), *Perspectives on socially shared cognition* (pp. 349–364). Washington, DC: American Psychological Association.

Romiszowski, A. (1997). Web-based distance learning and teaching: Revolutionary invention or reaction to necessity? In B. Khan (Ed.), *Web-based instruction* (2nd ed., pp. 25–32). Englewood Cliffs, NJ: Educational Technology Publications.

Rosenberg, D., & Sillince, J. (2000). Verbal and non-verbal communication in computer mediated settings. *International Journal of Artificial Intelligence in Education, 11*, 299–319.

Rossner, R., & Stockley, D. (1997). Institutional perspectives on organizing and delivering Web-based instructions. In B. Khan (Ed.), *Web-based instruction* (2nd ed., p. 333). Englewood Cliffs, NJ: Educational Technology Publications.

Rourke, L., Anderson, T., Garrison, D. R., & Archer, W. (2001). Methodological issues in the content analysis of computer conference transcripts. *International Journal of Artificial Intelligence in Education*. Retrieved July 10, 2006, from http://communitiesofinquiry.com/documents/2Rourke_et_al_Content_Analysis.pdf

Rowntree, D. (1987). *Assessing students: How shall we know them?* (2nd ed.). London: Kogan Page.

Rowntree, D. (1995). Knowing our learners in ODL. In *Block 1 overview essay of H804 study guide* (pp. 27–47). Milton Keynes, U.K.: The Open University.

Rowntree, D. (1998). The role of workshops in staff development. In C. Latchem & F. Lookwood (Eds.), *Staff development in open and flexible learning* (pp. 231–238). London: Routledge.

Rowntree, D. (2000). The implementation of open and distance learning. In *Open University H804 study guide, block 1, knowing our learners in ODL* (pp. 8–23). Milton Keynes, U.K.: The Open University.

Sewart, D. (1998). Tuition and counselling: Supporting the teachers for competitive advantage. In C. Latchem & F. Lookwood

(Eds.), *Staff development in open and flexible learning* (pp. 148–156). London: Routledge.

Sharpe, R., Benfield G., Lessner, E., & DeCicco, E. (2005). *Scoping study for the pedagogy strand of the JISC e-Learning Programme*. Retrieved March 12, 2007, from http://www.jisc.ac.uk/uploaded_documents/scoping%20study%20final%20report%20v4.1.doc

Smith, J., & Osborn, M. (2003). Interpretative phenomenological analysis. In J. Smith (Ed.), *Qualitative psychology* (pp. 39–45). London: Sage Publications.

Smith, P., & Ragan, T. (1997). Web-based instruction: What is it and why is it. In B. Khan (Ed.), *Web-based instruction* (2nd ed., pp. 5–22). Englewood Cliffs, NJ: Educational Technology Publications.

Taylor, J. (1997). *Flexible learning systems: Opportunities and strategies for staff development in industry*. Australia: The University of Southern Queensland. Retrieved December 2006, from http://www.usq.edu.au/users/taylorj/readings/aaou.html

Thorpe, M. (1994). Planning for learner support and the facilitator role. In F. Lockwood (Ed.), *Materials production in open and distance learning* (p. 146). London: Paul Chapman.

Thorpe, M. (2000). Learner support: Planning for people and systems. In *Open University H804 study guide, block 3* (pp. 51, 59). Milton Keynes, U.K.: The Open University.

Thorpe, M. (2001). *Rethinking learner support: The challenge of collaborative online learning*. Retrieved March 12, 2005, from http://www.scrolla.ac.uk/resources/s1/thorpe_paper.html

Tight, M. (1988). Defining distance education. In *Open University course guide H801 ICDE bulletin* (Vol. 18, pp. 55–60). Milton Keynes, U.K.: The Open University.

Tudge, J. (1989). *When collaboration leads to regression: Some negative consequences of socio-cognitive conflict.* Paper presented at the International Conference on Computers in Education, Taipei, Taiwan.

Vygotsky, L. (1978). *Mind in society: The development of higher psychological process.* Cambridge, MA: Harvard University Press.

Wegerif, R. (1998). *The social dimension of asynchronous learning networks.* Centre for Language and Communication, School of Education, The Open University. Walton Hall, Milton Keynes, MK7 6AA, 34–47.

Yin, R. (1993). *Applications of case study research.* London: Sage Publications.

FURTHER READING

Bannan, B., & Milheim, W. (1996). Existing Web-based instruction courses and their design. In B. Khan (Ed.), *Web-based instruction* (2nd ed., pp. 381–387). Englewood Cliffs, NJ: Educational Technology Publications.

Bassey, M. (1999). *Case study research in educational settings.* Milton Keynes, U.K.: The Open University.

Boling, E., & Frick, T. (1997). Web-based instruction: Holistic rapid prototyping for Web design—Early usability testing is essential. In B. Khan (Ed.), *Web-based instruction* (2nd ed., pp. 319–327). Englewood Cliffs, NJ: Educational Technology Publications.

Boyle, T. (1997). *Design for multimedia learning.* London: Prentice-Hall.

Boyle, J. (2002). *Learning lessons from MLE development projects.* Retrieved October 12, 2006, from http://www.jisc.ac.uk/uploaded_documents/ACF681.doc

Brusilovsky, P., Schwarz, E., & Weber, G. (1997). Electronic textbooks on the World Wide Web: From static hypertext to interactivity and adaptivity. In B. Khan (Ed.), *Web-based instruction* (2nd ed., pp. 255–260). Englewood Cliffs, NJ: Educational Technology Publications.

Bunnell, D. (2000). *Making the Cisco connection: The story behind the real Internet superpower.* New York: John Wiley & Sons Inc.

Bush, V. (1945). *As we may think.* Retrieved January 12, 2005, from http://www/theatlantic.com/

Cochran-Smith, M. (1995). Uncertain allies: Understanding the boundaries of race and teaching. *Harvard Educational Review, 65*(4), 541–570.

Cotton, J. (1995). *The theory of learning.* London: Kogan Page.

Duchastel, P. (1997). Motivational framework for Web-based instruction. In B. Khan (Ed.), *Web-based instruction* (2nd ed., pp. 179–184). Englewood Cliffs, NJ: Educational Technology Publications.

Durbridge, N. (1998). Interaction in multimedia. In *Knowledge network internal document KN1156* [article posted by the tutor to the H804 conference area]. Milton Keynes, U.K.: The Open University.

Farish, M., McPake, J., Powney, J., & Weiner, G. (1995). Equal opportunities in open and distance learning. In R. Mills & A. Tait (Eds.), *Supporting the learner in open and distance learning* (pp. 129–144). London: Pitman Publishing.

Gleenie, J. (1996). Towards learner-centred distance education in the changing South Africa context. In R. Mills & A. Tait (Eds.), *Supporting the learner in open and distance learning* (pp. 19–31). London: Pitman Publishing.

Gold, R. (1969). Roles in sociological field observation. In G. McCall & J. Simmons (Eds.), *Issues in participant observation* (pp. 30–39). Reading, MA: Addison-Wesley.

Hannum, W., & Briggs, L. (1997). Incorporating interactivity and multimedia into Web-based instruction. In B. Khan (Ed.), *Web-based instruction* (2nd ed., p. 41). Englewood Cliffs, NJ: Educational Technology Publications.

Harasim, L. (1990). *Online education: Perspectives on a new environment.* New York: Praeger.

HEFCE. (2005). *Consultation on HEFCE e-learning strategy.* Retrieved October 29, 2006, from http://www.hefce.ac.uk/pubs/circlets/2003/cl21_03.htm

Hitchcock, G., & Hughes, D. (1995). *Research and the teacher* (2nd ed.). London: Routledge.

Holmberg, B. (1977). *Theory and practice of distance education.* London: Routledge.

Jennings, M., & Dirksen, D. (1996). A process for adoption of Web-based instruction: Facilitating change. In B. Khan (Ed.), *Web-based instruction* (2nd ed., pp. 111–116). Englewood Cliffs, NJ: Educational Technology Publications.

Khan, B. (2006). *Flexible learning in an information society.* Hershey, PA: Information Science Publishing.

Kuehn, S. (1994). Computer-mediated communication in instructional settings: A research agenda. *Communication Education, 43*(2), 171–183.

Leidner, D., & Jarvenpaa, S. (1995). The use of information technology to enhance management school education: A theoretical view. *MIS Quarterly, 19*(3), 265–291.

Ligorio, B. (1997). *Social influence in a text-based virtual reality.* Unpublished master's thesis, University of Geneva, School of Education and Psychology, Switzerland.

Mason, R. (1991a). Methodologies for evaluating applications of computer conferencing. In A. Kaye (Ed.), *Collaborative learning through computer conferencing* (pp. 2–5). Heidelberg, Germany: Springer-Verlag.

Mason, R. (1991b). Moderating educational computer conferencing. *DEOSNEWS, 1*(19). Retrieved July 8, 2008, from http://www.emoderators.com/papers/mason.html

Mason, R., & Kaye, A. (1989). *Mindweave: Communication, computers, and distance education.* London: Pergamon Press.

Moore, M. G. (1995). The 1995 Distance Education Research Symposium: A research agenda [Editorial]. *American Journal of Distance Education, 9*(2), 1–6.

multimedia. (n.d.). In *Rane professional audio reference.* Retrieved March 2003, from http://www.rane.com/digi-dic.htm

multimedia. (n.d.). In *What is? Dictionary.* Retrieved December 2006, from http://whatis.com

multimedia. (2008). In *Merriam-Webster online dictionary.* Retrieved July 8, 2008, from http://www.merriam-webster.com/dictionary/multimedia

Nunan, T. (1994). *Analysing technology in educational settings: Distance and open education in Australian higher education.* Paper for the XII International Conference on New Concepts in Higher Education, Melbourne, Australia. Milton Keynes, U.K.: The Open University.

O'Donnell, A. (1996). Effects of explicit incentives on scripted and unscripted cooperation. *Journal of Educational Psychology, 88*(1), 74–86.

Oliver, M. (1999). *A framework for the evaluation of learning technology* (ELT Rep. No. 1). London: University of North London.

Prebble, T. (1988). If they play as mean as they talk: Some implications of the 'user pays' approach. *Distance Education, 9*(1), 116.

Rasmussen, K., Northrup, P., & Lee, R. (1997). Implementing Web-based instruction. In B.Khan (Ed.), *Web-based instruction* (2nd ed., p. 341–346). Englewood Cliffs, NJ: Educational Technology Publications.

Ross, B. (1993). What has happened to convergence? In T. Nunan (Ed.), *Distance Education* (pp. 114–138). Adelaide, Australia: University of South Australia.

Schon, D. (1987). *Educating the reflective practitioner*. Presentation to the 1987 meeting of the American Educational Research Association, Washington, DC, transcribed by Jan Carrick, January 1998, posted by Tom Russell, Queen's University, January 1998.

Shannon, C., & Weaver, W. (1949). *The mathematical theory of communication*. Urbana, IL: University of Illinois Press.

Vygotsky, L. (1997). Incorporating interactivity and multimedia into Web-based instruction. In B. Khan (Ed.), *Web-based instruction* (2nd ed., pp. 231–232). Englewood Cliffs, NJ: Educational Technology Publications.

Wegerif, R. (1988). The social dimension of asynchronous learning networks. *Journal of Asynchronous Learning Networks, 2*(1), 493–516. Retrieved July 25, 2004, from http://www.aln.org/alnweb/journal/vol2_issue1/Wegerif.pdf

William, V., & Peters, K. (1996). Faculty incentives for the preparation of Web-based instruction. In B. Khan (Ed.), *Web-based instruction* (2nd ed., pp. 107–110). Englewood Cliffs, NJ: Educational Technology Publications.

Woolley, D. (1996). *Guide to conferencing on the WWW*. Retrieved August 30, 1988, from http://freenet.msp.mn.us/~drwool/webconf.html

Yamane, D. (1996). Collaboration and its discontents: Steps towards overcoming barriers to successful group projects. *Teaching Sociology, 24*(4), 636.

Zimmer, B. (1993). The empathy templates: A way to support collaborative learning. In Lockwood (Ed.), *Open and distance learning today* (pp. 142–145). London: Routledge.

INDEX

Index

44, 49, 51, 63, 100, 102, 141,
152
instructional, 65, 67, 100, 104,
125, 130, 150, 152
design, 28, 65, 104, 152
dialogue, 54
environment, 49
material, 150
instructor, 6, 27, 39, 65, 74, 105,
136, 159
integration, 47, 52, 88
intellectual, 34, 49, 55
interactive, 6, 8–9, 11, 38,
47, 55, 59, 65–67, 76,
89–90, 96, 100, 103,
125–126, 133–134,
136–137, 141, 151, 158
learning, 66
video, 47
interactivity, 67, 105, 136, 152
interface, 6, 16, 28, 139–140,
151, 153–154
interface design, 6
international, 15, 82
Internet, 14, 17, 27–28, 47, 64,
73, 100, 104, 106–108, 110,
130, 138–139, 141
Internet service provider, 64
interpersonal, 9, 27, 38, 57, 59,
64, 163
interpretive, 14, 78–79, 92
intranet, 3
isolation, 25

jobs, 38, 45–46, 55, 119,
122–123, 162–163

journal, 10, 15, 140
just-in-time, 43, 123

knowledge worker, 48

layout, 139
learning
activities, 65, 97, 119, 143
contract, 100
material, 22, 40, 74, 80, 154
learning methods
network, 13, 65–66
paths, 43, 138
resources, 53, 117
styles, 32, 44, 56–57, 162–163
support, 9, 11, 143
theory, 49
lecturers, 34, 46, 52, 56
lessons, 23, 29
library, 37, 73, 102, 111, 124,
137, 140
listserv, 156, 162–163
literature, 7–8, 21, 30, 62, 67–68,
73, 77, 94, 143, 145, 158

market, 2, 15, 27, 29–30
Martin, 123
meetings, 14
mentor, 38, 42, 46, 52, 63
metacognitive, 75, 116
Microsoft, 52, 90–91, 106–107,
129, 136, 145
multimedia, 9, 16, 26, 105, 125

navigation, 16, 55, 98, 136–137,
139
needs analysis, 143